AF414095

Living Without Bubble Wrap

Mary Encinias

ISBN (Paperback) 979-8-3302-9945-4
ISBN (eBook) ISBN: 9798878219686
1. Mary Encinias - Nonfiction   2. Childhood Disease – Nonfiction
3. Osteogenesis Imperfecta – Nonfiction
4. Healing Journey – Nonfiction
5. Memoir – Nonfiction   6. Surviving Fractures - Nonfiction

Printed in the United States of America

Book and Cover Design by Joan Kellogg

Before You Begin

Recently I sent a birthday card to a friend. It was a design I had colored with pencils, but I left part of the card uncolored in order for her to complete. I felt it demonstrated our connection although we were hours apart, we were one in spirit. My friend loved it and happily showed me the results.

In the same way, my story is not complete. I have penned things that I have experienced while living with *Osteogenesis Imperfecta,* or "brittle bone disease." It's a genetic mutation that makes your bones fragile.

I'm not sure why you picked up this book. You may have a disease yourself or are the parent of a child with OI. Whether your bones are fragile or not, we are all seeking wholeness. This book will take you along my journey from getting out of PE in school to finding yoga in my forties, from needing my mother to comfort me as we drove to the Emergency Room one more time, to swimming laps on my lunch hour. It will show you the importance of support for the child who gets left out.

I had aunties that wanted to put me in bubble wrap. Once I got new Mary Jane shoes to wear for Easter. While visiting aunties that afternoon, one of them took my shoes and scraped the bottom of them so I wouldn't slip. They didn't do that to my sister's new shoes. Everyone wanted the best for me and for that I'm thankful.

But incidents like that were reminders that I was different when all I wanted was to live life to the fullest. It was not fun to have a fracture almost every year, but what I have learned could come no other way.

In addition, my story engenders hope. A rare medical disorder does not define me, nor does a medical diagnosis or feeling different define you. The diagnosis of Osteogenesis Imperfecta was a blow to my parents, but hope abounds. I have endured over 65 fractures while enjoying a full life, rarely slowing down.

I have broken many bones, but not my spirit.

Like the birthday card for my friend, there are parts of my life still uncolored. Turn the pages and help me to finish with satisfaction.

Full speed ahead.

Note to reader: This memoir comes from my recollections and journals. Some of the language reflects the word usage at the time, such as "crippled" instead of "disabled." Additionally, client names have been changed to conceal their identities.

Living Without Bubble Wrap

Table of Contents

Before You Begin

Part One: Fragile, Handle with Care

Part Two: People Who Need People

v

Section Three: A Soft Landing

Part One: Fragile, Handle with Care

1

It Has a Name

I shall gather up the fragments of my life
and make a crazy quilt of them.
Or a mosaic of interesting patterns –
unity in diversity. This will be an adventure.
Agnes Smedly

These first fragments of my life came from stories told by my parents and siblings.

They say I was born on the hottest day of the year in Elyria, Ohio in 1953. The hospital A/C was broken. Mom was there in labor for the sixth time, but she was a trooper. Daddy waited outside where he could smoke. I came into the world around four o'clock, September first, a new month, a new daughter, named Mary Monica. When Daddy went home to tell the rest of the kids, they were happy with the news. A new little sister!

I was named Mary Monica because of Mom's Uncle Peter. He was a priest in Wisconsin and very dear to my mother. He had always encouraged her studies throughout her childhood and hoped she would enter college after high school because of her good grades. However, being a poor farm girl that didn't happen. I was to be named "Peter," but because I was a girl, I was named after the church Uncle Peter built in Whitefish Bay, Wisconsin, St. Monica's.

Six weeks later, I had my check up with the family doctor. Mom told me about it many times. She was admonished by Dr. Sullivan after he examined me. "What have you been doing to this child?" She answered, "Just loving her. I'm breastfeeding as well." He knew our family well. My Dad worked for an ambulance service part time, so was known by many doctors.

Mom had known Dr. Sullivan since her fourth child, Rita, was born. Dr. Sullivan stated "She has a broken arm and possibly some fractured ribs! See how her right hand droops? It tells me the bones and muscles are not working together. This could be serious."

"What?" My Mom was dumbfounded. "What do we need to do?"

"I'll call Rainbow Babies and Children's Hospital in Cleveland and get you an appointment to see an orthopedic pediatrician right away. I can't put a name to it yet, but this Mary Monica has some sort of bone or muscular condition."

"Thank you, Doctor. We'll be careful with her until then."

Mom told me she went home and waited for my dad to get home from work at the Steel Mill in Lorain. It was a long afternoon and finally he came through the back door carrying his thermos and lunch pail. Mom took him aside and told him the bad news. The appointment in Cleveland would be in two weeks.

After examining me, the specialist in Cleveland pronounced the words, *Osteogenesis Imperfecta*, meaning 'bones from birth are imperfect'. He pointed out that the sclera of my eyes had a bluish tint. That was one of the diagnostic features. Mom said her heart started to race and holding daddy's hand he grabbed his smelling salts. They had never heard of that disease. It was rare. Mom told me hearing the news was like being hit in the chest with a baseball. She hardly heard the next words the doctor said. Life expectancy was unknown. There was no known cure. They were told my bones were fragile and fractures were to be expected. There were no medications that could make me stronger. I could roll over and break a bone.

"What can we do for her?" Daddy said.

The doctor told them to make a pillow sized board of plywood and to cover it with a pillow and pillowcase. I had to be held and carried on this pillow board. He cautioned them to not let the other kids hold me. He wasn't sure if I would ever walk. He said they'd have to just wait and see. I imagine my parents walked back to the car in total shock. What would become of little Mary Monica?

During the thirty-mile drive back home from Cleveland, with tears in their eyes, my parents discussed plans and how they could best make preparations at home for me. There was no need for hospitalization at this point. They would be careful, and no one else would handle me. There was Aunt Dolly, Nana, my dad's sister and mother, and others in town who could help with the other children. People were already praying. Although sad, my mom and Dad were hopeful. They were in this together, Dad knew something about health care, and everyone would rally around them. They would love this child and she would have a good life.

Being devout Catholics and strong in their faith my mom suggested that they stop by their church, St. Mary's, and talk to their pastor. Fortunately, Monsignor Newton was in the church praying. They entered the dimly lit sanctuary. One candle is burning in a red holder signifying the Eucharist was present. Monsignor Newton listened, his twinkling blue eyes showing concern as they poured out their hearts to him. Prayers, being a part of everyday life, were requested, prayers for healing and strength. He invited them to place me on the altar dedicated to Our Lady. Putting his hands on me and offering his blessing he recited the beginning of the Gospel of John:

> *In the beginning was the Word. And the Word was with God, and the Word was God. He was in the beginning with God. All things came to be through him, and without him nothing came to be.*
>
> *What came to be through him was life, and this life was the light of the human race; the light shines in the darkness, and the darkness had not overcome it.* John 1: 1-3

Mom told me that she and dad were comforted by the sincerity of his understanding and the prayer. They felt something significant, maybe even holy, had happened. They knew Monsignor Newton had been a scripture scholar before his assignment to St. Mary's, and one of his accomplishments was the translation of the Gospel of John from the original texts. They trusted him immensely. He appeared to share their sorrow, but he spoke of light coming from darkness. Somehow, they would have to rely on their faith to make peace with this news.

Back at home, my sisters told me my parents shared the diagnosis with the whole family. Marg became emotional and sat down heavily on the couch. For all of them it was a horrible shock. They knew Becky Graham, two doors away, who had cerebral palsy, but this was a disease they hadn't heard about. Daddy got to work cutting plywood. He was glad there was something he could do to help. Mom instructed the others what was required; that I would be carried on the pillow board and that we would do the best for little Mary. As for the future all would have to be patient with waiting to see what developed and continue to pray,

I have an old black and white Christmas photo showing me as a happy baby. Another photo shows Jim, 14, Marg, 12, Anne, 10, Rita, 6, and Tommy, 4 surrounding me with the pillow board settled on a footstool. A contented smile indicates I was comfortable and pain free. My adventure, which had started out so hopefully, would have many bumps in the road, but I would always have the support of a loving family. Thus started my life without Bubble Wrap.

2

First Fracture

One who is at peace can draw good from everything.
Gerald Groote

Humpty Dumpty sat on a wall. Humpty Dumpty had a great fall. And all the king's horses and all the king's men couldn't put Dumpty together again. I wondered about him. I was like that; I could fall and end up in a million pieces. I tried to put it out of my mind most of the time, but there were times I was afraid.

Year by year my bones would break and twist and grow and break again. The pain would be almost constant yet being different would expand my vision to see different horizons and uncharted paths. By the time I was ten years old I had broken my right arm ten times. Each time the doctors put me back together again. I was no Humpty Dumpty!

On my birthday in 1956 we said goodbye to our house on Broad Street and moved to a Polish neighborhood in south Elyria. I was three. We moved into the house where my father had grown up. His mother no longer needed the large home, so she moved to an apartment closer to church and downtown. Daddy turned the large pantry near the kitchen into a downstairs bathroom so that I would not have to climb up to the second story for the bathroom.

We all liked the new house on Twelfth Street. Our house was a three-story frame less than a mile from downtown Elyria. We had a big front porch and a full unfinished attic and basement. The attic was hot in the summer and cold in the winter. On the second story, the three girls slept in one bedroom. The two boys, Jim, and Tommy had a room together, and I had a bedroom of my own. The girls' room looked out onto Twelfth Street through a large bay window. A painting of Saint Theresa hung on the wall in their room above the radiator. Flowered wallpaper gave way to painted walls in the 1960s. Another religious icon stood on my parents' dresser, a large statue of the Sacred Heart of Jesus. Our parents were typical Catholics for that time and that place. No meat on Fridays. No movies during Lent. My mom dressed me in blue on every Mary Feast Day to honor the Blessed Mother. Saturdays were for cleaning, and the older girls had to work, or they could not see their friends that evening.

My Mom and Dad, married in 1938, wanted a big family and said they were 'blessed' with six children. Dad had work at the steel mill in Lorain, Ohio, throughout the depression and the war. There had been steelworker strikes and illnesses, but they had weathered those storms. We prayed together as a family before meals and on Sundays at St. Mary's Church. And we prayed the rosary together as did a lot of Catholic families during the 1950s. Marg told me that I learned to walk holding on to the footstool, going round and round, while everyone else kneeled in various places in the living room.

Our lives were as predictable as a deck of cards. All of us girls were preparing for marriage and children. Women's' lib had not surfaced in Elyria, Ohio yet. But I was different. In my mind, something was wrong. I do not want to be falling. I do not want to hurt. *I do not want to be picked up. I do not want to be carried.*

I do not remember when I first knew. I do remember the bathtub. As a toddler, the warm water felt good. I soaked away the pain. I played. I dreamed. I was free in the water. Naked. Alone or with my brother, Tommy. The worst part was getting out of the tub. I did not want to be picked up under the arms and lifted. It did not hurt but I felt scared and slippery. I could fall. Would I fall? More pain? More fractures? Hitting the floor with a thud, a crack, a scream?

I do remember my first major fractures a couple of months after we moved to Twelfth Street. I was jumping on the bed –

two beds in the girls' room tempted us. Any child would have done what we did; jump from one bed to the other. My brother Tommy, seven at the time, did it. I did it. We both giggled with joy. We found an exciting new game. Then it happened. I slipped off the corner and landed hard on the floor. My arm broke in three places. I would never be the same again.

I have *osteogenesis imperfecta* the brittle bone disease. My bones break like fresh saltine crackers.

Mom said I screamed a scream a mother knows is real trouble. I remember that moment. The sun shone through the sheer curtains. The hardwood floor beneath me. My father's comforting arms picking me up. The fear and pain. The long wait in the Emergency Room. This would be the first of many trips to the E.R. for broken bones. The orthopedic doctors did the best they could. They wrapped the arm close to my body. The swelling was bad; the elbow could not be set until the swelling went down. I was in tremendous pain. I saw my brother Tommy when we got home. He looked sad. He was there when it happened. He was fine. I spent the evening surrounded by pillows on the couch, eating ice cream.

The next day my arm hurt, but I walked around all bundled up, heavy with bandages on one side. I could not put my right arm into clothes. In a month or so, the swelling went down, and they placed my arm in a plaster cast. The bones healed but the elbow never bent again. It took three more years for my arm to be normal size and in that time, the elbow stiffened. By the time I entered kindergarten, my arm was in another cast because of yet another fracture. When the cast came off my arm was straight, with a slight curve in the forearm. My fingers and wrist moved well. The doctors did not have any better ideas of how to mend it, so they left well enough alone.

By that time, Mom and Dad were learning of other children with osteogenesis imperfecta who were much worse off. A small support group was formed for parents of the children with OI. My mom never attended any meetings but read the newsletters which came in the mail. OI, although a genetic condition, had never surfaced in any other family members. In my case, it was a spontaneous mutation. I was just fragile. I had to be careful but was active and happy. We all lived day by day, being careful in ice and snow. No other special accommodation was needed.

One Sunday in church, with the scent of incense floating in the air, I saw a girl in front of us staring at me. I knew she was staring at my crooked arm. It was springtime and the sleeves on my dress were s short exposing my arm. I turned to my mom and indicated I did not like it. Mom said, "She's just looking at your beautiful blue eyes, honey. Don't worry about it." I considered what Mom said. I turned my attention back to my missal and followed the Mass.

Even then as a five-year-old I did not like how I looked. I was not only small but skinny as well. My teeth were crooked, so I felt disappointed with my looks. I did have blue eyes, though. I wanted what everyone else wanted; cool clothes, straight bangs, and to be as pretty as a flight attendant someday. Would my day ever come? I watched my older sisters dress up for proms and met their boyfriends. They are strong and athletic. I was not. I was scrawny. I could barely hit a whiffle ball. They took tennis lessons and had their pictures in the paper. I colored pictures of dogs and homes on hills. I prayed the rosary with earnestness hoping one day I would stop breaking my arm. They said all my bones were fragile, but I just kept breaking this one arm. Why me?

I needed a stamp on my forehead saying, FRAGILE, HANDLE WITH CARE.

3

Family Antics

*All the variety, all the charm, all the beauty of life
is made up of light and shadow.*
Leo Tolstoy

As is its fashion, life went on and the shock and worry over my bone disease blended into the usual cares of family life. I overheard my mom and Dad talk about concerns such as: *Would Jim, my older brother, be responsible enough to have his own car? Could we afford a summer vacation?* I was a curious little girl, so I listened in on conversations, even though I seemed preoccupied. There were five children who needed attention, not just me.

Our family had four teenagers in the house, so things were never dull. I relished all the commotion; teen parties before and after football games were always fun. We made confetti from old newspapers and packed bags of it to toss at the football game. And there were school dances. Margaret and Anne shopped for dresses and Mom altered them. The music of Johnny Mathis played over and over on the hi-fi.

All of us attended Catholic school at St. Mary's and Elyria Catholic High School. Mom, who always wanted to be a teacher, helped with homework and projects. She drafted poems, built dioramas, and went over spelling words with each of us. The nuns at St. Mary's knew our family well. Dad and Mom were chosen "parents of the year" once.

Not all of us were diligent students, however. Here is an incident that garnered a lot of attention in the household. When Tommy was in eighth grade, my parents went to the school Open House to meet with his teachers. Sister Mary Andrew, a sister of

Notre Dame of Chardon, Ohio, drew them aside, "I would like to show you your son's book report."

They looked at what she pulled out of her desk drawer. It was a short paragraph about the book, *The Rise and Fall of the Third Reich*, by Louisa May Alcott. Miss Alcott did not author that book, and Tommy had not read her book, nor the one he reported on.

My parents were so embarrassed! They made apologies to Sister and said they would work harder with him at home. Tommy, four years my senior, was often in trouble. He liked to cut up, make people laugh. He was good at sports and was lots of fun, but school was not his "thing." His favorite show was The *Three Stooges* — not exactly an intellectual pursuit.

There was something else my sisters talked about. Once Jim, fourteen years my elder, had too much to drink at a wedding reception. He was new to the world of drinking and came home late wobbling and weaving. The whole family was asleep. He was as sick as a dog and ran upstairs to what he thought was the bathroom. The three girls asleep in the front bedroom awakened with a jolt! Jim had turned right instead of left at the top of the stairs, believing it was the bathroom. A Windsor chair with a skirt and removable padded seat was in the corner. He lifted the cushion as if it were a toilet seat and vomited the contents of his churning stomach into the chair. Marg, Anne, and Rita screamed, awakened by such a noise and smell! Jim was never allowed to forget that night.

And finally, there was an event that we all shared. One snowy February day in 1959, the whole family went sledding. A blizzard had brought over six inches of snow to our small mid-western town. School was closed. The snow was hard-packed on the sledding hill in Cascade Park, making perfect sledding conditions. Daddy brought the old wooden sleds from the garage and piled them in the car. On that cold blustery day, Mom and I had watched the kids slide down the hill over a dozen times when Mom had an idea.

"Try it with Rita on the sled lying on her stomach and Tommy, who was smaller, lying down on top of her!" They were twelve and ten years old. Tommy was game. Rita agreed. They glided down the smooth, icy snow. As soon as they got up to speed, another child, oblivious to all but the wonderful snow, walked right in front of them, dragging his sled behind. Our sled hit the other kid's sled with a bang. Rita and Tom spilled onto the hill, a crush of bodies and ice. The distracted boy had cleared the coasting sled, but they hit his sled. There was blood!

Rita's mouth slammed into the boy's sled. They rushed her in the car to the hospital where it was revealed that she had injured her jaw and lost four teeth. Daddy stayed with her at the hospital while Mom took me and Tommy home. Rita was treated and released, but the incident loomed large in my mind for years. Poor beautiful Rita — at the young age of twelve she had braces on her teeth! Tommy was unscathed, as he was a tough one who took his scrapes and bruises with ease.

I felt so bad for Rita, for I knew what it was like to be hurt and bandaged up. I waited at home, remembering all my trips to the Emergency Room. The high-up ER bed, covered with stiff sheets; pillows covered with plastic that crinkled. No real comfort, just survival. I would lie on the bed waiting, waiting for the doctor, waiting for the x-ray people to get me, waiting for the x-ray to be read. I was not alone. Mom or Dad was always with me. And even when the waiting stopped it was no better. The Doctor would take my hand and ask me to squeeze his finger. Ouch! I just could not squeeze like before. Then he would take my arm into his big fleshy hands and twist it.

The x-ray table was always cold and hard. The room was dark, and they had me place my broken arm on the table propped this way and that way for the x ray. I could only feel pain and fear, and tears rolled down my cheek.

But this time it was not me. It was Rita. And there was blood. Never did my broken arms produce blood! All my own breaks made me more sensitive to the suffering of others.

I didn't want people I loved to hurt.

4

First Grade

*Love is the fellow of the resurrection, scooping up
the dust chanting, "Live!"*
Emily Dickinson

It was 1959 and time for me to enter the first grade at St. Mary's School. It was a tradition in my family to have a new dress for the first day of school. I wouldn't be ready until I had the right dress. Our Catholic school didn't require uniforms. My Mom found time, between ironing curtains and talking on the phone, to take me shopping. I'm thinking now she didn't know how hard it was going to be.

We went to a big department store, but I was turned off by all the pastel dresses on the rack. We tried another dress shop. I thumbed through the rack of clothes, skirts, blouses, dresses but nothing pleased me. For some unknown reason, I had something in mind that would be serious enough for first grade yet perky to match my personality. We had to abandon the search that day without buying anything.

The big day was getting closer, but I had nothing to wear. *What was Shirley Temple without her tap shoes?* I was worried. We had to go out shopping again. I was tired and cranky. There was a store out on the highway called "Robert Hall." My older sisters had found *Bobbi Brooks* sweaters and skirts there. Let's try it! The somewhat daunting row of dresses in my size, 6x, loomed long before me. I slowly looked at each one. And then, there it was! A black and white jumper, over a white blouse with a red bow. The material was a plaid in the hound's tooth pattern. I could see myself going to the head of the class in that one.

We finally found the one and only frock suitable for that auspicious day, the first day of first grade. Now, I'd be able to start my adventure in learning. Now, I can carry my books like the big kids, complain about homework, and fill my lunchbox with bologna sandwiches and grapes. It is said, "Once you have the dress, the occasion will present itself." And it did.

That first day of school was a whirlwind. We sat in rows of desks. Sister Mary Margaret Stephen was our teacher. She was young and energetic as she passed out our supplies of scissors, paper, and a small box of letters on squares we could use to form words. Oh! I will soon be reading! The readers had big words and pictures of children running. I was in my glory! And for once, I wasn't the smallest girl. Donna Wade was even shorter than I was. John DeMarco was a flashy boy with a bright smile who wasn't afraid to speak up. My heart skipped a beat, my first of many infatuations.

We had to form a line to travel to the cafeteria at lunchtime. Boys and girls were wiggling in line across the wide expanse of parking lot to get to the Marian building where the cafeteria was in the basement. The tiled room was enormous and noisy with big kids. It smelled of oranges and cookies. Chairs scraped the floor and wax paper crackled as everyone opened their lunch bags. My lunch box was full. I sat with a friendly girl, Janie, who was next to me in line. We talked, acutely aware that our teacher was watching us. Before I knew it, the bell rang, and we were expected to leave again. I did not have time to eat my lunch!

It was going to be a good year. I had arrived! I went home to tell my family about each boy and girl. My dress was perfect. When my dad came home from work, I climbed up on his lap and told him I would be writing my name soon. He held me close knowing what was ahead.

The crowded school playground scared me. I didn't want someone to knock me over. I was afraid of breaking my arm again. After a few weeks, someone decided I could only go to school for a half day so that I could rest in the afternoon. I had to accept it. I don't remember Mom or Dad asking me about it. I went home at lunchtime and Mom made me go to my room and take a nap. But I wasn't tired. I lay there and thought about school. I was being treated differently because of my bones. Nobody else wanted me to break my arm again either. I understood that. I was six and my right arm had been broken four times already. So, I did what I was told. I tried to rest. But I didn't like it.

My room was painted lavender, which was my favorite color at the time. My double bed took up most of the room. I had my dolls, my books, and a window facing the backyard. I covered my bed with pillows like I still do, trying to be comfortable. I held on to my wiggle bunny as I looked around and tried to figure out things. I thought about Jesus and Mary and Joseph, hoping I'd have a family too, someday. I lay there until the smells of supper cooking wafted up the stairs.

Finally, the last day of school arrived in June. I was allowed to go for the whole day and enjoy the party. We also brought in rags to clean our desks. I felt happy as a first-grade graduate! On the way out to the car for the ride home, I tripped over a rock and hit the ground hard. Everyone heard me scream. I knew that familiar feeling. I broke my arm.

Daddy lifted me as gently as possible into the car and I clutched the broken arm close to my body with my good arm. Tears ran down my face, and everyone thought it was the pain. Yes, it hurt terribly, and I felt each bump and crack in the pavement as the car maneuvered down Fourth Street, but the tears were for anger and frustration. I hadn't had a chance to enjoy the triumph of my first-grade graduation. I hadn't had the chance to share my good report card with my brothers and sisters. I was on my way to the hospital - again.

The pain of a broken bone, how can I describe it? At first it is a sharp, stabbing pain, and you cannot move that limb without a pang. I was afraid someone might bump into me. Only when the doctor came did I release the arm for his exam. Then he ordered x-rays. The tech wheeled me down the hall to the x-ray room where I'd have to get out of the wheelchair and onto the table. Always, always, the table was cold. The room was dark with little me, the x-ray tech, and the big machine. The tech tried to be friendly and fast. She slid heavy metal plates into a slot in the table. She measured the distance between the little light on the machine and my arm. She knew I was in pain, but by then, I wasn't crying. I was watching every move she made. She left me to use the machine from another room, telling me to hold my breath. I heard a small beep and waited again. If the picture came out okay, I was wheeled back to the Emergency Room to wait for the doctor. I was happy to see my mom.

Sometimes they would give me pain medicine, so that by the time a cast was put on my arm, I could stand it. But the drive home was difficult as the movement of the car jarred my arm. I slept that afternoon; I slept to forget how long the summer would be with a cast on my arm. Upon awakening, I started to count the weeks ahead. I yearned for the day my cast would come off. Each time we visited the orthopedic clinic, I wanted them to plug in the circular saw and cut the cast off. I had to wait a long time, about six weeks. And when the cast finally came off, my arm was weak for several weeks.

This was my life. It makes me different. It makes me strong. I can muster through pain like a linebacker who goes back into the game. I can empathize with people suffering from the pain of cancer or other illnesses that cuts them off from others. Sufficiently resilient, despite the costs.

Everyone has something. I have this.

First Grade

5

The Doll Hospital

Staying inside while the other kids were outside riding their bikes, I imagined different places to live and houses with wide front lawns. I loved dolls. In the earliest years I had baby dolls with plastic painted hair and cloth diapers. I took good care of those babies and never left them on the porch or unprotected. They slept soundly with me as I took the required afternoon nap. They looked to me for love.

When I had a cast on my arm it was harder to manipulate them or change their clothes. So, I started collecting dolls on birthdays and Christmas that were, well, just to look at. One was the bride doll, and another was the Shirley Temple 'Rebecca of Sunnybrook Farm' doll. How sweet they were, perfectly styled hair, never a wrinkled dress. The dolls made me smile even if I was alone. In my mind I could run and jump like Rebecca of Sunnybrook Farm. Another favorite was my bride doll. I imagined, while I was supposed to be napping, strolling down the white carpeted wedding aisle in the long white dress.

The broken arms were disruptive to my play, but I managed. I had older brothers and sisters to watch, TV, puzzles, and books. I related to *The Ugly Duckling* and dreamed of being pretty one day. *The Little Engine That Could* taught me to keep on trying when things were difficult. And one story was about a little girl with sore legs who took up ballet and became a ballerina. I wanted to be a ballerina, too. Mom got me a tutu for Christmas, but I only put it on once because I felt embarrassed about my skinny legs.

Dolls were my true love. One day a box arrived in the mail. I opened the box and found a new doll in a blue dress in a box labeled, "Maribelle, the Doll who gets well."

What a wonder she was. About a foot tall, with curly brown hair, she came equipped with stick-on measles and chicken pox, tiny stickers of red and yellow. When you put them on her face, she was sick. When you took them off, she was well. And to top it off, she had two plaster casts-one for her arm and one for her leg. These came on and off, too. She had to play more gently when she had a cast just like me! She had to cover her cast with plastic when she took a bath, just like me.

We all enjoyed Maribelle. She was with me on the couch if I had to miss school. She went in the car on errands with mom and me, and on vacation. She always wore a smile. My smile wasn't sculpted in plastic, but I tried to be cheerful, despite the falls and breaks. I learned to tell jokes. Adults laughed at my jokes, and I laughed, too. I also had a big doll that was three feet tall. If you lifted her right arm, she took a step. She had curly short hair. Soon I asked to get a perm, so I could look more like her. And then, my mom made us both dresses out of the same material! We were a sight! I named her Caroline, after President Kennedy's daughter.

Another fine day, my grandma, "Nana" drove me to a town nearby. Nana was a seamstress, and sewed fancy clothes for ladies and sometimes for dolls. She took me to a place outside of town where she had mended some dresses for antique dolls in the shop. Outside the big sign said, "Doll Hospital."

Inside the lighting was dim, but the counters were filled with dolls of all kinds. There were dolls with faces of china, Raggedy Ann dolls, many more bridal dolls and babies. The man behind the counter was quiet and kind. I knew he had to be the doctor. My blue eyes filled with tears as I thought of all the broken dolls. He was a miracle worker. Nana gave him the dress she had sewn, and he thanked her. We continued to look around and saw all the repaired dolls waiting for their owners. I vowed to be more careful with my dolls. Although it was a nice place, I just did not want any of my dolls to have to be in the hospital, away from home. I was thankful that a place like this existed. We said our goodbyes and headed back to our house.

For years after that first visit, my heart was in my throat whenever we drove by The Doll Hospital. It left me feeling tender inside for the broken dolls, never thinking that I, too, was one of them.

Doll Hospital

6

Uncle Fred

Uncle Fred wrote his name in Chinese on my cast. Laughing, telling jokes and playing tricks on us, he was everyone's favorite uncle, and he had a way of making each one of us feel like we were his favorite. He was actually my mother's uncle, the brother of my grandma. He was a Catholic priest and had been a Maryknoll missionary in China. These memories are from the early 60s, he was living in Glen Ellyn, Illinois teaching Latin and Greek in the Seminary.

Once our family took a vacation to New York to visit the headquarters of Maryknoll, a Catholic Missionary Group. I think it was for the anniversary of Uncle Fred's ordination to the priesthood. What I saw was a giant collection of buildings with touches of Chinese architecture painted a bright red. There was a large mission bell and several chapels. In one of the dining rooms, we were invited to a dinner in honor of Uncle Fred. It was a fancy affair.

But our Uncle Fred was not that priest in China, he was the one who would sit with us and play Parcheesi. He was just a great guy. In those days, he wore the old-fashioned cassock, which is a long black dress with lots of buttons. It had a white collar designating he was a priest.

And he prayed a lot! We would see Uncle Fred reading his breviary in the morning or just before bed. He told us that a priest had to read the prayers in that book every day. It was one of the rules.

Uncle Fred visited us in Ohio a couple of times a year. He

also visited relatives back in New York City, the brothers and sisters of my grandmother who didn't move to Ohio. He had the first movie camera we ever saw. He took movies of the relatives in New York and showed them to us and vice versa. He had been doing this since the 30s when my mom was young.

We loved looking at the old black and white movies. Once he showed us movies outside at my grandfather's farm. It was not of relatives, but a mission movie showing a woman cutting sugar cane with a machete. The picture on the screen affected me deeply. She fell during her work, and I felt so sorry for her. At night before sleep I thought of people who lived in other places having to grow their own food and do work like that woman cutting sugar cane. I wondered if I would ever go to a place like that. *Would I be able to keep up?* Yet it was so far away from Elyria, Ohio. *How brave of Uncle Fred was to work so far from home.* We also had two missionary nuns in the family, who worked in South America. They brought the outside world to us, letting us know there were other ways to live.

At home we often played like we were nuns and priests. We had a nun outfit that I wore. My brother, Tommy, dressed in all black, like a priest. He was a real altar server, so had to learn some Latin phrases. He brought home his laminated card of Mass prayers. The words were funny to us, and even with repetition, we barely understood. We pronounced the words phonetically and played at being pious and sincere until someone saw us, and we would burst into laughter. I think I even baptized a few Protestants in my backyard pool. Our family was Catholic through and through. If my sisters even dated a non-Catholic, Aunt Theresa would have something to say about it. It jeopardized their gift money at graduation or Christmas.

Uncle Fred was a hero for all the thirty-four cousins who lived in Ohio. He gave us money every Christmas. It was a grand affair! He would enter the room at my grandma's house with a stack of envelopes. Then he'd call out our names and we would go up to him and receive the gift, just like he was passing out report cards. The older you were the more money you got. Even my naughty brother, Tommy got a nice sum. He never missed any of us. And Mom taught us all to write Thank You notes to him after the holiday. Aunt Theresa, who lived in Oberlin in the old family house, did the same. But she wasn't as much fun. She had never married and was a bit on the crabby side. But we thought they were both very rich giving out all that cash.

Years later I learned more about Uncle Fred's work in China. He was there in the days before the communist revolution. He helped to build schools and even a Catholic Seminary in Southern China. Things were primitive at best. They didn't have electricity or running water. They had to care for the sick since there were no hospitals, all the time keeping to their duties of the priesthood, saying Mass and sharing their faith. Everyone loved Uncle Fred, but I was the only one with my name in Chinese on my cast!

He was an incredibly organized man. When he died and they emptied his file cabinet, they found folders for many of the relatives. One folder had my mom's name on it. They mailed it to her. Inside she found every letter she had ever written to him, from high school all the way until his death. Of course, I looked for my birth announcement. What I found was a hand-written note to him from my mother. It said, "we regret to inform you that our Peter was born and her name is Mary Monica." We all had a good laugh over that one.

Me, my cousins and Uncle Fred

7

"I Feel Pretty"

"I feel pretty! Oh, so pretty! I feel pretty and witty and gay!" sang Maria in *West Side Story*. We listened to Broadway show soundtracks at our house and I sang along. Sometimes I belted the words out like Ethel Merman and other times I sang as softly as Julie Andrews. I related to the tender sad songs like "Goodnight my Someone" from *Music Man* and "Climb Every Mountain" from *The Sound of Music*. My heart as soft and sensitive as a kitten, I could see in my mind the beautiful Broadway stars coasting about the stage. I was one with them, dancing and falling in love.

Being the youngest, I watched as my sisters got dressed for dates and talked about boyfriends. I couldn't wait to get one of my own. Mom, for her part, was busy preparing the four of us for marriage. We learned how to make our beds; she told us the neater we made the bed, the more handsome our husbands would be, so I ran back to my room and tucked my bedspread in more neatly. When peeling an apple, we were instructed to make the peel one long strip and keep it connected. Then she told us to throw it over our shoulder and the shape of the apple peel would be the first letter of our husband's name. Marg and Anne seemed to have dates every weekend. Dresses, corsages, dyed heels to match the dress were the stuff of my dreams.

"Oh, Daddy, do you have to use those bright lights?" we cried. He had a movie camera and took pictures of the girls coming down the steps with their prom dresses. The light set he used must have been thousands of watts. They tried to smile, but they were also squinting their eyes in most home movies. And I wanted to be in the pictures, too. At times, I stood in front of the girls posing with them.

29

Besides my sisters, Jim was quite popular with girls. Jim was a handsome guy with shining brown eyes and wavy hair. After high school graduation, he worked at a local factory making plastic duck decoys. His easy smile caught the attention of a cute little waitress at a coffee shop in Elyria. Her name was Jan, from West Virginia. She was so tiny compared to my sisters and wore size five shoes. I had never met anyone from West Virginia with an accent like hers. She said "Y'all!" After a while it was clear Jim had found his one and only and they would be married in a June wedding. Mom set out to plan the wedding because Jan's parents still lived in West Virginia. Jan and her three sisters had been sent up to Ohio to make it on their own when they were teenagers. Well, this time Jan really hit the jackpot – she met my brother! And they were getting married.

The wedding plans included a Catholic Mass at St. Mary's and an evening reception at the local Polish Club just two blocks from our home. Our neighborhood was full of Polish people, and we knew the place well for their fish fries on Fridays. Jim and Jan discussed everything with mom and dad. One evening at dinner Jan asked me to be her flower girl! "Mary, will you?" she said.

"Oh, yes! But what am I supposed to do?" I asked.

"You walk down the aisle of the church before the bride and carry a basket of flowers" She encouraged me.

"I can do that."

"Marg and Anne will be bridesmaids. Tommy will be an altar boy. And we're asking Uncle Fred to say the Mass," Jan continued. "All the dresses will be light blue."

The time seemed to drag as we waited for the big day to come. Mom made the big girls' dresses. My dress was store bought but fit just right. The June morning arrived with sunshine, fresh air and frenetic activity. We went to the YWCA for photos before the service. Jan was living there temporarily. I was sad that her own parents wouldn't be there, but we were going to be her family now. Jan looked like a little doll in her wedding dress. I couldn't believe I would be a part of this fairy tale.

Then it was my turn to shine. We arrived at the church and got assembled in the back, out of the view of friends and relatives who had already arrived. Uncle Fred was there to officiate. Of course, the bride was the most important woman of the day, but I felt the light of attention shining on me too. My long blue taffeta dress flared out with a hoop slip beneath. The ruffles went from the waist to the floor. And happily, I had no cast on my arm.

I felt like a princess in that frock. I walked slowly down the aisle of the church with a big smile, holding tightly to the basket of flowers. After the church part of the wedding, the wedding party went to a photographer's studio to pose for formal pictures. Everyone was in blue, adorned with flowers and flanked by young men in black and white tuxedos.

And I was in nearly everyone! It was like being a movie star. No one noticed my crooked arm. Shy at first, but within time I felt that I belonged in front of a camera.

At the reception everyone danced to the live band music. I learned to polka. I danced with my dad and cousins. Aunts, uncles, and friends seemed filled with joy. I ran around the Polish Club with the other kids and took home a piece of wedding cake wrapped in a napkin. We were told to put the cake under our pillows so we would dream of the man we were to marry. I was so tired, ready to dream of that special wedding day. I placed the cake under my pillow. But when I awakened, I had no memory of dreaming anything. I resolved to try another night or two. In time, the cake dried out, never giving me the answer, I so dearly wanted. But I had glided through our first family wedding and emerged a pint-sized beauty.

I Feel Pretty

8

In the Newspaper

I liked the feel of daddy's whiskers when he held me, and I believed he knew everything. My Daddy always knew what to do in emergencies because of his training in First Aid and working for a funeral home part time. In those days funeral homes had ambulances to transport sick people, sometimes in emergencies. When I broke my leg for the first time, his skills were put to the test.

It happened one gorgeous April day. I was running across Twelfth Street but the public space between the sidewalk and the street had been dug up because the city was working on the sewer. Well, with my lack of coordination and strength, I tripped over the clods of earth and took a big fall. My right leg was broken, I knew.

Daddy came running and as he assessed the situation. A large lump grew up on my leg and I began to cry. Daddy said, "Looks like you broke a blood vessel, sweetie along with the bone. I'll get you to the hospital."

Others outside came to join me. Daddy came out of the house with a leaf from the oak dining room table. He placed it under my leg and went to get the car. Along with Mom's help, he slipped me with the braced leg into the back seat of our car. I would soon be in the ER again with a new fracture. I was familiar with the routine. Wait. See Doctor. X-ray. Cast. This was my first leg cast. The cast went from my foot to my upper thigh, and it was heavy! And right in the middle of my shin, a little hill in the plaster, to accommodate the broken blood vessel. To me it was hideous. *I couldn't go back to school like this! My life was over!*

Time passed and the pain subsided. I sat outside on the

chaise lounge and read books and colored. I was never alone. Both Mom and Dad were strong enough to carry me upstairs to the bedroom at night, cast and all. Friends came to play every few days. I got through it.

At the same time, my brother continued with his paper route and faithfully delivered the Cleveland Plain Dealer every morning. He let me help him count the money he collected, mostly coins each week. The Sunday paper was big, and he had to stuff the ads and comics into the newspaper which arrived Saturday in the middle of the night. Sometimes I helped him with that, too. He had a manager from Cleveland who collected the money. He would always visit and joke with me, since I was usually home, lying around like Cleopatra in my leg cast.

Just as things were going well, things changed. While sitting on the chaise lounge, I shifted my weight, leaning on my right arm too much and broke the arm again. Another cast! Now I was a two-cast freak. With time, the pain wasn't too bad so I returned to quiet playtime to wait until I would be free to run and play again. Waiting. Boredom.

But then something cool happened. Tommy's newspaper manager brought a reporter with him to interview me for a story. I told him about *Osteogenesis Imperfecta* and all my broken bones. He listened to my story and my grade-school jokes. It was easy enough. He sent a photographer on another day, so we were prepared. I loved the attention. Friends who came to visit that day were included in the photo shoot. We didn't really know how and when it would be in the paper.

The paper arrived on May 9, 1964. Tommy woke us up running through the house yelling, "Mary's on the front page!" The headline above the fold was impossible to miss: "Bad Breaks Mar Life for Mary" I was the talk of the town. The photo showed Tommy pushing me in the wheelchair and another one with my friends lined up on the couch. I was famous! Mom and Dad were proud.

Because of my notoriety, I began to receive letters in the mail from people who wanted to send their good wishes and start corresponding with me. One older man sent me his photo which was kind of weird. But with nothing else to do, I began corresponding with some of them. I was flattered that a boy from Sandusky, nearly 80 miles away, wrote to me. He was my age and lived near Cedar Point, a big amusement park. *Maybe someday I'll meet him,* I thought. I'll never forget those letters.

Since then, I have always loved letters. And postcards came from all over Ohio. I weathered this predicament of a cast on my arm AND my leg with joy. I had lots of names on both casts. I could not be sad.

9

Gain and Loss

It is in the shelter of each other that people live.
— Irish Proverb

"Rescue squad? Yes, right away!" I heard Mom say. It didn't register in my mind what those words meant. I thought it had something to do with Rita because she had a job at Elyria Memorial Hospital. I was not alarmed until I went into their room and saw my Daddy gasping for air. Mom said, "Go back to your room and say some Hail Marys."

It happened three days after my sister Anne's wedding. With the Viet Nam war raging, Anne and Denny were married in June 1964 in order for Denny to avoid the draft. He had a good job working with his dad as a roofer, and they planned to get married in October. But with the draft board letter in hand, he would get a deferment if he were married, so they decided a June wedding was better.

Then came the morning I woke up to the sound of Mom on the phone calling the hospital. My room was across the hall from my parents' room. I went back to my bedroom. *"Hail Mary, full of grace, the Lord is with thee…"*

Tommy, Rita, and Marg were awake now and went into Mom and Daddy's room. They saw what I saw: Daddy, our big, strong father, struggling on the bed and Mom holding his head in her hands. She asked Rita to run down the block and get our brother, Jim. Married to Jan with a son of his own now, they lived in a small house also on Twelfth Street. Rita, still in her bathrobe, ran down the street.

I felt scared. I knew my dad had a heart attack a year ago but he was doing fine, so what had changed? I prayed, *Blessed art thou among women and blessed is the fruit of thy womb, Jesus."*

Jim ran up the stairs. We were all there – Jim, Marg, Rita, Tommy, and me. Anne was on her honeymoon. The Rescue Squad people came up the stairs, rushing, but it was too late. My Daddy had taken his last breath. Mom came to me and thanked me for praying.

We all wandered downstairs to the living room. The emergency responders took their equipment with them and left. Then the funeral home people came to carry my dad's body out of the house. We knew these men because Daddy worked part-time at the funeral home. It was June. No school. Summer. And now our Daddy is gone. He wouldn't get to enjoy his long, fourteen-week vacation from the steel mill. The sadness was palpable, leaving an empty space in my heart. Tears came. It was so quiet. No TV, no one getting ready for work or school, no one even getting dressed. All of us were stunned.

This day, unlike my mood, was sunny and clear. Our telephone got a real workout that day. All day long Mom was either calling someone, or someone was calling us to offer their support and love. And there was the problem of finding Anne.

It was Tuesday. On Saturday Anne had been a beautiful bride. She married her sweetheart, Denny, who was from Pittsburgh. We had the wedding reception at our house. Daddy had worked so hard getting our yard ready with its roses, snapdragons, petunias. It had been a perfect day.

Earlier in May, I had casts on my leg and my right arm. But I was feeling okay now. Anne wanted me to be in the wedding. Our local paper had done an article about us: Anne, the future bride and me, the optimistic little sister, hoping to get my casts off for the wedding. There was a photo of me with my casts and Anne looking over a piece of material for my dress in the local newspaper. Two weeks before the wedding I had my regular cast-check appointment.

"I'd like to be in my sister's wedding. Can you take my casts off please?" I said to Dr. Strong.

"We'll see what we can do," is what Dr. Strong said to me in his gruff voice.

Dr. Strong then took the circular saw and ran it up and down my arm cast. I was free!

"There now, you'll look pretty in your dress. But the leg cast must stay. We'll turn it into a walking cast."

A compromise. I was sad, but I eventually understood. Maybe I won't walk down the aisle, but I'll be in the wedding.

June 13, 1964, had been a great day! We have loads of pictures to show for it. Anne wore a mantilla for her veil which was quite fashionable. Mom made a junior bridesmaid dress for me. After all, I was ten years old, too old to be a flower girl. The dress was pink and long enough to cover the leg cast. All my cousins were at the wedding, and we had a good time playing around and posing for pictures.

But here we were just three days after that wonderful occasion. We had to find Anne and Denny. We knew they were headed to the Pocono Mountains in Pennsylvania. Denny's parents suggested we call the Highway Patrol of the State of Pennsylvania and have them look for their car. We gave them the license number and description of the car. It took a while, but the Pennsylvania Highway Patrol found them on the turnpike and pulled them over. They were told to call home. It was after dark when the phone rang at our house. Mom had to tell Anne about Daddy's massive heart attack that took his life.

Anne and Denny turned around and headed back to Ohio. Anne told us years later how she had just collapsed in the phone booth hearing the news. It was a shocking blow to hear so far away from home. Just in their early twenties, they had to begin their marriage on this low note; all the happiness of Saturday, dashed by Tuesday.

For three days, we were caught up in the cloud of grief. People brought food and tried to help Mom. Then we dressed and went to the funeral home, where my dad had worked, and saw him lying in the casket. It seemed like everyone in town came to see us. We were embraced and loved.

My Daddy was only fifty-three years old, and my mom was forty-six. I didn't know then how much this early loss would impact me. Almost everything in our lives was about to change.

"Holy Mary, Mother of God, pray for us sinners now and at the hour of death. Amen."

Anne's Wedding

10

"I'm not crippled!"

*In separateness lies the world's great misery;
in compassion lies the world's true strength.*
Gandhi

After my father died, my mom and I grew very close. I had a cast on my leg that first summer without him. It went all the way from my toes to my hip, but at least I could at least get around on my own without crutches. I really hated crutches. They take up room, they are heavy, and I didn't really feel secure with them. The plaster cast was just big and clunky. On the bottom of the cast, there was a strong rubber anchor, so to speak. It allowed me to walk. But I still felt isolated from the kids riding bikes in the neighborhood, and I felt sad for my mom.

Mom was still in shock, I guess, over the death of my dad. She had never worked outside the home and was desperately trying to find something to do and bring in a little income. Marg, my oldest sister, was still home, having finished college. She was working for the welfare department. Rita and Tommy were in high school. Their interests took them out of the house, so many days, it was just me and Mom at home.

It was the summer after my fifth-grade year. The Beatles were all the rage, and I was one of their biggest fans. I collected Beatle cards, trading cards with their photos and facts about them. I copied how to do each one's signature. I kept myself busy around the house. I guess that is one thing I learned by being laid up all the time. I know how to entertain myself. I read Nancy Drew mysteries. Nancy was so smart! She unraveled crimes and her lawyer Dad answered her legal questions. *I wished I had my dad.* I drew with crayons on clean white paper scenes of my dream house. I wanted to live on a hill, and my house had to have a picture window. I thought our house was quite ordinary. I didn't like ordinary people; I wanted to be special, famous even. I watched Patty Duke on TV. She played two parts, herself, and her cousin from Scotland. I thought the show was quite clever; she changed her hair and her speech and became a whole different person.

My friends, Rosette and Cindy, would come over to the house and visit. We could play Barbie dolls or a board game. But it was summertime and I longed to go swimming. Hamilton Elementary School was across the street from our house. The playground had monkey bars, swings, and box hockey. Even though we didn't go to that school during the school year, it belonged to us when school was out. I spent a good deal of time on the front porch just staring, too.

Mom came out of the kitchen wiping her hands with a towel. I was alone in the living room. She sat down. "Mary, would you like to go to camp this summer?" she said.

"What camp?" Just the thought of it made me curious.

"There is a special camp for crippled children called Camp Cheerful," she replied.

My heart stopped. *What was she saying? That I was 'crippled? No way!*

"Mom, I'm not crippled!" tears forming in my eyes.

"I just thought you might like it instead of sitting around here all the time," she said.

"No. No. No! I will not go!" Mom turned around and went back to the kitchen. I sat there fuming. *What did she think of me? That I would be like those kids in wheelchairs? That I wasn't normal? That I had to be put in that kind of group? No, I was just like everyone else, I thought. So, even if I had a broken arm or leg once in a while, that didn't make me crippled.*

I was so mad, I couldn't speak. I sat there and cried, looking at the cast on my leg, hating everything about my life and about my mom. She just didn't understand.

It never came up again. A movie played in my mind showing kids in wheelchairs sitting around a picnic table with adults. I didn't mind disabled people; I just didn't fit in with them. I was stronger than that. I could sing, put on shows in the garage, draw, and tell jokes. I had a lot going for me. I didn't want to be put in a 'special' category. *Thank God! So, I couldn't ride a bike or play jump rope this summer. I'd survive.*

The resentment about Mom's offer of Camp Cheerful didn't last long. My brother Tommy came in with his paper route money and let me help him count it. Soon we were making piles of nickels, dimes, and quarters on the rug. No, I wasn't handicapped or disabled. I was Mary Monica, a perky blonde with plenty of life ahead of me.

11

Child's Play

Mom was still in shock over the death of my dad. She had never worked outside the home and was desperately trying to find something to do and bring in a little income. Maggie, my oldest sister, was still home, having finished college. She was working at the welfare department. Rita and Tommy were in high school. Their interests took them out of the house, so many days it was just me and mom at home.

I spent a good deal of time on the front porch just staring, too. Another one of my favorite places was the attic. I'd go up there. The attic was a special, albeit dusty, place of ancient dresses, piles of books, and yellowed newspapers. If I went up to the attic on sweltering days, then I could come back down the steps and the house felt cooler. Everyone's house was alike on our street. No one had air conditioning.

I thought about my dad. Before he died, we would visit my dad at Bittner-DeCarlo Funeral Home when he was on duty, but only when they didn't have a body. During that time, the funeral people provided ambulance services as well. My Dad had to transport people alive or dead.

Elyria was a small town with one hospital, so my dad seemed to know everyone there. He was a friendly guy. After his death, his wake was held at the same funeral home. Many people came to see our family over the space of two evenings. We were united as a family standing in front of the open casket. He was well respected in the community for his church involvement, his work, and for being a father of six. But the funeral home wasn't totally somber. We laughed and told stories, although I'm sure I saw tears being wiped from faces with fancy handkerchiefs. What the friends and relatives saw was the six of us children standing with my mom. And me, ten years old, sporting a large cast on my leg.

Daddy was in a fancy casket wearing his best suit. They placed a rosary in his hands. He had his glasses on, I guess, to make him look like himself. Tommy and I noticed the lacy pillow under his head and giggled a little. He had brought a couple of those pillows home to us once and we would have nothing to do with them. There were lots of baskets and vases of flowers. I noticed one card with a flower arrangement that said "WCQT." Later that night at home I asked Mom what those letters stood for.

Mom laughed and said, "That's my ladies' group. We are five Lutherans and five Catholics who have been friends for years. Since we didn't have a name for our group, we just called it "WCQT" for We Can't Quit Talking. We both laughed.

I remember standing there at the casket for hours. A few of my fifth-grade friends came to greet me and that was nice of them. The funeral Mass was at St. Mary Church. Mom bought a cemetery plot near where our Uncle Hank was buried. He died the year before. As a young girl, I thought it was strange that my mom and my aunt Dolly had their names already on the stone when their husbands were buried. The stone had the year of birth and death. John Wirscham 1910-1964. Gertrude Wirscham 1917-19 . In time, we would have to change that to 2015.

In the weeks that followed the funeral, I watched my mom write dozens of thank-you notes for all the kindness shown to us during our time of grief. The funeral home had given her boxed thank-you notes. Those flat white boxes, when emptied, became my Barbie doll house furniture in the corner of our living room. They measured about four by six inches. I put three boxes together, side by side, to make a modern couch. Other boxes came in handy to serve as a coffee table and chairs. Barbie and Ken sat around discussing her new car on white sleek furniture. Then they changed clothes again. This house was always neat. No one messed it up.

It was ironic to turn something from the funeral home into a child's play. My daddy had died. We were all shocked and sad. Our large extended family embraced us and friends came to call. My ten-year-old mind could not contain the tragedy. I held my body stiffly and smiled. I was waiting to get my leg cast off.

I had the best Barbie doll house of all my friends, and I kept all the clothing ensembles together. I coped. I overheard Mom talking to people about looking for work. She didn't have any real skills that I knew of. She tried doing telephone survey work because she loved to talk on the phone. I had to be quiet when she was on the phone. If mom got a job outside the house, I wasn't sure how that would work. I heard things about moms who went to work, but I couldn't imagine my mom doing that. I didn't want a working mom.

But Barbie and Ken kept up appearances. They looked good in the thank you note house. They thrived. Mom had to do jury duty. It was complicated. She kept moving forward. I spent the time in my corner of the living room at Barbie's house. Our house was quiet, but Barbie's house was full of life.

Mom went about her duties with the same energy she approached all things. Don't stop. Keep moving. Things will get better. She had been a farm girl. She had enough strength to endure. Her legs were almost always in support hose. It seemed she never stopped. Mom's shirtwaist dresses were not fancy like Barbie's, but she looked fine to me. She watched daytime TV shows about people with problems. On the soap operas there were divorces, affairs, people who lied, and people who cared too much about money. Our only problem was that mom lost her husband and my daddy was dead.

But Barbie still had Ken. This one thing was for sure.

12

The Girl on the Swing

Twelfth Street was the center of my universe. When you grow up in a big family, you must find places where you can be alone, away from the ringing phone, the television, the bouncing basketball.

My place of reverie was the front porch swing. It really wasn't a swing, but an upholstered glider. It hung on a chain so you could sit, legs kicking from the floor or lie down, feet tapping the short end giving a lighter bump, bump, bump. On long, hot, summer afternoons you'd find me there. I faced the street, but because of the awning, couldn't be seen by passersby. Like a heartbeat, my foot caused the swing to beat in rhythm with whatever pop song was stuck in my head. Sometimes it was "Cherish" by The Association or "These Boots are Made for Walkin'" by Nancy Sinatra. Cars glided by kids on bikes, but I was somewhere else. *What would I be? Would that cute boy ever call me on the phone? Why are some plants called weeds and other flowers? Would I ever gain weight?* It seemed like I ate all week with no results. The oak leaf hydrangea waved in the breeze. Mom pointed out to me that the flowers start out a pale white then gradually turn to pink, then rose. Time passes. The hydrangea guarded our porch. What makes it last through the winter? Like forsythia, it comes up every year. I wondered about these things.

Curiosity was my constant companion. I investigated my sisters' vanity drawers and found makeup and a leaflet about menstrual periods. I wondered about what the nuns' house might look like, but I never saw inside. That was always to remain mysterious. One year during Trick-or-Treat we walked all the way to the convent on Fourth Street to get their treats. I had heard that the cookies they gave out were very good. Well, on the way home, drat! My bag was stolen by bigger kids running by me.

The front porch was also a good place to read on quiet days. Nancy Drew books taught me to use my mind to figure things out. She was such a brave woman! She figured out where the hidden staircase was. She examined things like clocks and garden gates. She was blonde and blue eyed just like me. Her father was a lawyer, no mention of her mom, but they had a housekeeper. My father was a steel worker, and my mom cleaned our house. But there were other things we had in common. She was confident and knew how to ask questions. So did I. I liked to interview people. I had to interview my mom about 'leisure' time once for a school assignment. Mom laughed out loud, "What leisure time?" Short interview that was.

Nancy Drew inspired the investigative side of me. I looked up boys' names in the phone book wondering where they lived. I read through old letters in the attic. In my adult life as a counselor for the State of Florida, I delved into people's lives to recommend to the court which parent should get custody of the kids in a divorce. It wasn't murder, but it was important. I took notes, just like Nancy Drew. I remembered things and observed people.

Every year I broke my arm - some claim to fame. In the summer before my sophomore year of high school I broke it at the beach. I felt so stupid! I was sitting at the water's edge just enjoying the gentle lapping of the waves of Lake Erie washing up on my tanned legs. The water came up to my waist, so I decided to push myself backwards up the sand. I leaned on my right arm, snap, the familiar sound and piercing pain. I broke my arm again!

I was alone on the beach, camping near Toledo, Ohio, with my sister Maggie and her husband Fred. They were back at the campsite. Somehow, I had to get up and go to them. I struggled to my feet, holding my arm, and slipped on my shoes. *Darn! Another cast!* I had taken sewing lessons this summer and just made a new dress, and I'd have to cut out the sleeve. *Oh no!* Tears fell from my eyes as I approached my sister, dismayed.

"Are you sure you heard it snap?"

"We're hours from home."

"Do you think doctors here would know what to do? "

"Maybe we should take you to the hospital where they know you?"

I got tired of having to 'train' the Emergency Room doctors who didn't know about *Osteogenesis Imperfecta,* so we decided to go back to Elyria. I guess I could make it through sophomore year with a cast on my arm. *It just wasn't fair.*

A few painful days later, I found myself back on the front porch swing. Reviewing the last few days in my mind, I tried to cheer myself up, but I was down in the dumps. *I will write my own life story I thought and call it "Break it to me Gently – the Girl on the Swing."*

52

13

Mary's Diary

As my journey without bubble wrap continued, nothing could protect me from broken bones or teenage angst. Even though elementary years included fractures and the death of Daddy, those years were also idyllic and I felt loved. I had friends and cousins who were kind and fun to be with. I had art projects and my interest in singing to keep me entertained. I also had a backyard pool, three feet deep.

But the teen years were different. Things were difficult for me. I was in high school at Elyria Catholic. I had friends who also came from large Catholic families but they had Moms *and* Dads. I only had my mom who was busy with her new job and church.

My sister, Rita, was in love. This was to the one. At age twenty, she was preparing for marriage. Her boyfriend, Tom, joined the Ohio National Guard to beat the draft. He went out of town for training, and she sent him Polaroid pictures of herself all the time. Her mind was elsewhere, so I couldn't talk to her. And Tommy was now enrolled at the local community college; he didn't give me the time of day. In fact, I think he was embarrassed to have me as a sister. But I idolized him because he could dance well and was the life of the party. So, I was lonely even amid people. So when I was about fourteen years old, I started to write down my thoughts and feelings in a diary. Writing helped me to unwind at the end of the day.

I was skinny. I had the same measurements as Twiggy, a hip new model from England. She wore bangs and short dresses. So did I, but I didn't look glamorous at all. I had orthodontic braces on my teeth! My arm was crooked from the many fractures; my right leg was bowed out a little below the knee because of a break. I had the occasional pimples. I tried hard to gain weight. I was sure I had a tapeworm. I ate and ate, but never gained a pound, weighing less than 100 pounds. I had no muscle tone. Other girls had muscular legs, but not me. Other girls had hips, but not me. I felt that I had nothing going for me.

At that time, all I really wanted was a boyfriend. Other girls had dates, but not me. I could be witty and relevant in class talking to boys, but when the bell rang, they scooted away, never pausing to carry on the conversation outside of class. At home, every time the phone rang, I hoped it was a boy calling. It never happened. I told myself they didn't know how to find my number in the phone book, because my last name was hard to spell: Wirscham.

Writing in my diary at the end of the day, sitting on my bed, I recorded my teenage misery: *"Thanksgiving. The church service this morning was okay. At the farm, everyone picked on me (as always). The dance was awful. Not one boy asked me to dance. Judy danced. She's okay. Donna and Tim just sat around. If that's what it is like 'going steady,' then forget it! I'm really down. I hate myself. Signed, Twiggy."*

I only had one arm fracture in high school, my right arm, but I still had pain even when I didn't sport a cast. Muscle spasms and bone pain were common. I took aspirin. My Mom rubbed Ben Gay on my shoulders. But I kept on smiling. I became an expert at hiding pain. Not to mention, I was such a people person that if I were with friends, nothing hurt. Distraction was my form of pain control. Although it was the late 60s and marijuana was not available, especially not in my circle of friends. That would come later. I smoked cigarettes behind closed doors, yet professed it was "bad for you" to my family.

Another diary entry from 1969 read: *"Went to the dance and no one asked me to dance. It was another heartbreaker. Cathy thinks she's too tuff for me. I don't even know what to do about tomorrow night. Maybe I'll go see the movie "Wait Until Dark." I'm very sad. Wirkner's band was pretty good. They only played two slow songs – thank goodness. I really wish I could just snap my fingers and be married, and all grown up and everything... signed, Twiggy"*

During this time, I made a new friend in David Gauchat. He introduced me to a new world I didn't know about. He was in my art class where Sister Mary Loren played Joni Mitchell music while we drew. It was a great class. We sat four at a table and were able to talk to each other while we worked. The friends I made in Art class would be my best friends. David was one of the boys I could talk to. David was tall and thin with a runner's build. He was on the Cross Country Team. He had nice blue eyes. He told me that his family took in handicapped children.

"Yeah, you know those babies with the big heads? We have some of them," he shared one day quietly, not boasting. Although David spoke to me in class, he wasn't demonstrative. I thought it was shyness, and later learned he was just uncomfortable in himself. He was talented in drawing. He made jokes, but they were kind of underhanded, like sarcasm. I found him interesting. Eventually, he invited me to follow the new highway out of town to the end, turn right and I'd be at his house. "You could meet the kids!" he added, figuring out I was the sensitive type.

I was indeed interested. I had read the book, *Angel Unaware*, by Dale Evans, wife of Roy Rogers. It was about a child born to them who was extremely handicapped and later died. That book moved me and my heart softened to children who were deformed or handicapped in some way. So, after getting permission from my mom, I drove one Saturday afternoon to "Our Lady of the Wayside."

I walked in the door at the side of the house and through a 'waiting room' of sorts. David came bounding down the stairs to greet me.

"So, here you are. This is my brother, Todd."

Todd had cerebral palsy and lived pretty much in this wheelchair. He wiggled in his chair and greeted me with a big smile.

He was a teenager, too. He couldn't talk so he had a lapboard with the alphabet on it. He used his finger to point to a letter; that's the way he told you what was on his mind. He also communicated with his eyes and smile. David got behind the wheelchair and wheeled it toward a steel door at the side of the waiting room and swung open the door. Behind the door was a long-carpeted ramp leading down to where the kids lived. David and his family lived upstairs, above the waiting room.

I followed them down the ramp to the newly built wing housing the handicapped children. At the bottom I saw a dozen young children playing, some of them in wheelchairs, some of them walking around. All were being watched by young girls in scrubs. Everyone seemed happy. It was Saturday and they had just finished lunch. I saw toys, books, a TV, all the things a kid would want. David pointed out a small girl in a tiny wheelchair with eyeglasses and introduced us, "This is Nina D., and she has OI like you."

"No kidding!" I was flabbergasted. She was so small. Then I remembered that some people with OI were dwarfed. They only grow about three feet tall their whole life, which creates other kinds of problems.

"Nice to meet you, Mary" Nina said. "So, how many fractures have you had?"

"I think about twenty, but it's hard to count," my smile widening. *Finally, another fragile person! She was younger than me, but maybe I could be a special friend to her.* I noticed her arms were both curved like my right arm. Her legs were so small; it looked like she never walked.

"How do you get dressed with that arm like that?" Nina asked, looking at my misshapen arm.

"I just put my arms in first, then take the top over my head," I replied, taken aback by this unusual request from an eight-year-old.

"Let's go, you two can talk later," David urged me on. He led me farther into the place, where I could see hospital beds, more children in wheelchairs, and the nurses' station. Turning right, there was a long hallway and then a closed door on the left. David opened the door and told me I could go inside. There were about ten cribs, each one occupied by a small child. There were two babies with hydrocephalus, or 'water on the brain' as lay persons called it, born with too much fluid on their brain. Some undergo operations which drain the fluid off with a shunt. These two babies, Medora and John, lived in these cribs. Parts of their heads were covered with towels for warmth because, as I was told, "their heads get cold."

The girl working in that room picked Medora up and held her for a while in her arms. A slight smile appeared on her little face. The young nurse seemed to really love her. Others were fed with tubes. One was very small, but I didn't ask what was wrong with each one. My heart was touched, and it was a bit over-whelming. There was music playing, bright colors, and beautiful sheets on their beds. A banner on the wall said, "Just to be is a blessing; Just to live is holy.' (Abraham Heschel) These children were seen as gifts from God, not children to be shuttered away.

In all I saw over twenty kids that day. I learned their names. Some could talk, like Nina, but most were non-verbal, but they reached out with smiles and gestures. Although my feelings were mixed with sadness, I knew how to connect with them. I took their hands, smiled and said something to each one. For once, I was the strong one and I realized I had love to share.

David seemed proud of the work his family was doing. He was certainly attentive to Todd. We took Todd to his room up the ramp and then went outside. David had something else to show me. It was a cabin in the wooded area behind the house. We went inside. It was like a hunter's cabin, with knotty pine walls and just a few pieces of furniture. He said, "This is my favorite spot. I come out here to get away from all the kids from time to time."

"How long have your parents been taking in these children?"

"Since before I was born. I don't know any other kind of family. It's just the way it has always been. They lived with us in the house until funds were raised for the addition."

"I'd like to get to know Nina better. Maybe we can talk about her interests."

"Sure. That would be nice."

Then it was time to go. I had a lot to think about on the thirty-minute drive home. *Where are their parents? How much medicine do they have to give them? What dedication by the staff! I want to meet David's parents someday. Maybe I could work there.* I learned that David's family, because of their association with The Catholic Worker, had begun caring for unwanted children in the 1950s. Their service just grew and grew into an agency called "Our Lady of the Wayside." The name comes from devotion to the Blessed Mother and love for those in our world who are left by the wayside.

There was nothing romantic between David and me. We were good friends. We were artists together, interested in the same things. We were both working on peace and against the war in Viet Nam.

One time, David really hurt my feelings. We were at the high school on Saturday for the homecoming parade. Before everything got started, I saw David in the parking lot and started running toward him. Distracted, I tripped over the speed bump and fell. Jumping up again, I was fine. No one else was around, David blurted out, "Maybe we should have left you at home with the crips." I smiled back at him, but that comment was insensitive. I never admitted what a slight he had just conferred upon me. *"I'm not a cripple!"* I screamed inside my head.

Yet, I was beginning to move out of childhood self-centeredness into caring about others. The visit to Our Lady of the Wayside helped me see beyond my own concerns, looking at the lives of those outside my family. I had been given everything, a large fun-loving family and security, yet there were those close by who didn't even have one parent.

I had a deep desire to make a difference in the world and to share my joy in life with those who had none.

59

14

The Change That Came

*The greatest revolution of our generation
is the discovery that human beings, by changing
the inner attitudes of their minds, can change the outer
aspects of their lives.*
William James

My world in the mid-sixties was small, mainly the neighborhood of Twelfth Street, St. Mary's School, and Catholic High School where my sisters and brothers attended ahead of me. We spent the holidays with our grandparents either on their farm or with my dad's family in Elyria. We had city and country cousins. We had three dairy farmer uncles, and my uncle, Charlie Brown, on my father's side, was an accountant.

Most of the people we knew were Catholic. We were Democrats. I had a colorful political button to wear in first grade. when Kennedy was running for president. At times, there were Democrat bumper stickers on our car. My grandmother worked at the voting booth on election days. My grandfather was on the school board for the Carlisle District Schools and active with the rural electric company board. Community involvement was a part of our family's story.

One afternoon, in the middle of a particularly boring day of seventh grade, our teacher brought up the Viet Nam War. She offered us names of servicemen who would like to receive letters from school children. It was 1966. I took a name and began writing letters to Juan Reyna on airmail stationery. I felt it was something I could do to support our country. I still have the letters he sent me, blue ink in cursive writing from my 'married' serviceman. When he ended his deployment, we stopped corresponding. That same school year, our teacher took a vote in class and asked us to raise our hands to learn who were "hawks" and who were "doves." That year most of us Catholic school children were "hawks." We believed we had to stop the spread of communism and Viet Nam was where the line was drawn.

At the same time in the South, the civil rights movement was in full swing. I heard about Martin Luther King, but we didn't read his books or hear his speeches. There were no non-violent actions staged in small Elyria as far as I knew. Down the highway, in Oberlin, Ohio, Oberlin College has admitted black students since 1835. Things were quiet in Elyria, but change was in the air.

It was 1967 when my mom went to work for the first time outside the home. It was then that we began to meet people of different races and faiths. My mom was employed by social worker Tom Peters* as he started a community-based corrections project in Elyria. He opened the first group homes for delinquent boys and girls in the state of Ohio. Mom had been in a group called Church Women United who were called upon to help set up the first girls' group home. Each different church took a room to decorate. The first home, called The Search, was located behind a closed religious goods store. Mr. Peters bought the store and reimagined it and turned it into an eclectic bookstore with posters, candles, and bead curtains. He hired Mom to be the store manager. The store was also called The Search and was across the street from Elyria High School. She worked at the store, mentored many of the girls, and it became her passion for the next thirty years.

To staff the group homes, Mr. Peters arranged to have conscientious objectors (COs) serve as counselors. COs were required to do community service for two years because they objected to military service, particularly the Viet Nam War, for religious reasons. There we started to meet all kinds of new people. Some were from traditional peace churches like the Church of the Brethren and the Quakers. There were even a couple of Catholics. One of the COs was Jewish. It was fascinating for me to meet people who were so dedicated to service to others. They left their families in other states and worked long hours with the kids in the group homes. There were women volunteers too, from the peace churches (churches that promote non-violence), who felt it was important to spend a couple of years doing community service.

More group homes were opened and the store grew larger and larger. By 1971, Mom was selling bell-bottomed jeans, hash pipes, and incense. It was still primarily a bookstore. Tom Peters ordered the books: *Soul on Ice* by Eldridge Cleaver, *Black Like Me*, by John Howard Griffin, *Man-child in the Promised Land*, by Claude Brown to name a few. I read many of them. Mr. Peters made sure the store had a strong psychology section with the latest titles. The Search was the place to pick up a gift from Berea College, Kentucky, or a rosary for your grandmother. It was a catholic bookstore, 'catholic' with a small "c," meaning universal and The Search was just that. With mom as the friendly and adept manager, she welcomed everyone from ministers to hippies. Each found what they were looking for.

I witnessed my mom unplug the coffee pot for ginseng tea and serve us Instant Breakfast mixed into milk. No more bacon and eggs. She embraced the volunteers and the children. She took a Gabriel Richard speaking course to give her more confidence in working with the public. She even participated in a transactional analysis group, looking at relationships based on the book, *I'm OK - You're OK*. She was becoming her own person, not just a wife or a widow. And she was very busy, leaving me to my own interests.

My bookshelves at home began to fill up with poetry anthologies and biographies of people who had made a difference in the world. I began to believe I, too, could make a difference.

I became a freshman at Catholic High in 1967. By 1970, most of the kids at Catholic High were "doves." The Kent State shootings were so close, just an hour away. Everyone was rallying against the war. My best friend Judy and I were hoping to attend Kent State after graduation. Practically speaking, Kent was an affordable state school. Judy's brother, Joe, went to Kent State and we looked up to him. He was in his dorm room when the May 4 shots rang out.

I attended anti-war meetings and tried to educate myself on the war. Jane Fonda came to town and spoke at the local community college. Jane Fonda was not respected in some circles because of her famous picture sitting on a North Vietnamese anti-aircraft gun. But she was a popular actress, so I was in awe. Right before her visit to Lorain County Community College, she had been stopped and searched for drugs in Canada. The camps dividing, people against the war were suspected to be drug-using hippies. The pills she had were all vitamins. After her presentation, people who wanted to be involved in the peace movement were invited to a local professor's house to plan actions.

My friend, David and I went to the professor's house in Eastern Heights for the meeting. I was star-struck, but inspired to do whatever I could to bring peace into the world. I remember clearly sitting in the living room of the well-appointed house. David asked, "So how do we get other kids in high school interested? Their only interest seems to be the latest football or basketball game!"

Jane Fonda answered, "Put a peace flier in the basketball program." I thought it was a great idea but could not fathom how we'd get permission to do that. Instead, I joined others to put together a small newsletter for peace. It was called "Write On!" We passed it out at school. We also wrote letters to our congressmen about the war.

There were peace marches in Washington, DC. I wanted to go so bad. I had a ride to go for a big march in April 1971, but in the end, I couldn't make it. I had come down with bronchitis. The cough was so bad, I broke a rib. This wouldn't be the first time my body thwarted my efforts to be all I wanted to be. I was so mad — imagine a hot rod without wheels; stopped in its tracks.

David and I had been in the same art class for years. We shared music tastes, youth retreats and the desire for the US to get out of Viet Nam. He was at Washington for the April 24 "March on Washington" and told me all about it. They had to sleep outside in a park, and I was green with envy. I still longed to be a part of something bigger than myself.

My world of Twelfth Street expanded to include concern for racism, war, and poverty. Mom and I volunteered at the local neighborhood center doing art projects with the children. My brother Tommy became a leader of a club organized to keep boys out of trouble. The kids were all black and, some believed if they had a club to belong to, it would keep them busy and give them direction.

It was indeed a time of change, and we were caught up in the wave.

Notes

*Tom Peters, founder of Betterway, Inc., my mother's boss, was indicted for twelve misdemeanor counts of sexually touching boys, twelve misdemeanors of asking to touch them and one felony count of taking sexual photos of a boy. He was found guilty of sixteen misdemeanors and confined in Lorain County Jail for eighteen months. (1988) This does not discount the hundreds of youthful offenders that were helped by Betterway, Inc. programs.

15

Surviving High School

Toward the end of high school, my social life improved. I still had no boyfriend, but I had friends. The cast came off my arm, the braces came off my teeth, and I was becoming a person people liked. On church retreats, I was known as the one who told the "Wide Mouth Frog" joke.

I was sixteen. Gasoline was cheap, thirty cents a gallon. One of our weekend activities was just driving around. We had our spots. One of us would get our parents' car. We had our circuit. We drove to Lorain down Broadway Avenue, the main street, dead in the evening, and waved at the old man who sat in front of his store. Then we'd go by the Big Boy on Erie Boulevard to see our friend, Linda, who dated "Diamond Jim" named after a sandwich. She'd join us to proceed farther west on Lake Road which went along Lake Erie's shore. At Lakeview Park we gazed at the fountain, lit up at night, and looked for people we knew. The park was perched high above the lake on a bluff. We didn't go down to the beach because of the dead fish, which did not make for a pretty beach. Our interest was in the people in the other cars. Usually, there were at least four of us; Linda, Terri, Anita, and me.

On those rare nights when we found no friends in the park, we drove out Gore Orphanage Road. The road was named for the old orphanage that was there in the early 1900s. Legend has it that the orphanage burned down, and all the children died. We were told that if we stopped our car on the bridge over the Vermillion River by the old orphanage, and turned off the car, we might hear the children crying. This was about ten miles from town on a country road. I had a tank full of gas, so we ventured out there one clear night.

The moon was nearly full, looking like a girl with her hair draped over the corner of her face. We could hear the summer sounds of crickets, cicadas, and mosquitos as soon as we turned off the radio. There was a cool breeze. No need for A/C in the car. The road curved to the left, then to the right. Placing my hands carefully on the steering wheel we finally came to the nearly indiscernible bridge. It was dark and hard to see. "That was it!" Anita called as we rolled on in the darkness.

"We'll have to find a place to turn around." We drove another mile before seeing a gravel driveway for an old farmhouse safe enough in which to turn the car around.

The chatter in the car continued, "Do you want to get some beer? I have my ID with me." Linda offered.

"No, not tonight." This was exciting enough. Although we sometimes got beer, it was too far back to town.

Carefully, we looked amid the trees and roadside growth, for the small bridge again. But now there was a car behind us so I wasn't sure I could stop. It was a couple of guys in a Pontiac GTO. They were right on our tails. "Speed up," Terri said. I took the car up to 55 miles per hour, but with the curves, I had to be careful.

"They're waving at us, slow down."

"Where you goin'?" the guys hollered out the window. They turned the light on in the car and I could see that the one on the passenger side was sort of cute. He had a bandana headband around his head and long hair. I could see him in the rearview mirror. I felt excited.

"Don't let them get ahead of us because they could block our car." Anita cried.

We continued this cat and mouse drive all the way back to the intersection with the Interstate where we had to stop. We locked our doors. The GTO zoomed around us, on to other things, and we breathed a sigh of relief.

We went back there another night and a similar thing happened; another car of boys, and a flirtatious fling down country roads outside a town where we knew no one. Excitement yet danger. We forgot all about the burning children at the old orphanage. Their bones merely a silent witness to our youth when gas was cheap and girls in cars kept the roads hot.

During the week, back at Elyria Catholic High School, I made felt banners for my ten nieces and nephews in art class - I was Aunt Mary, the one who would conquer the world. At Catholic High, I was asked to lead the senior retreats. That involved coming up with a theme, setting the tone, and making sure everything was set to give my classmates an experience of God. Although we were in a Catholic school and had religion classes, this was an opportunity to develop an individual spirituality, a relationship with Christ. I had no fear of speaking in front of others, especially about things that were important to me. My faith was something I wanted to share.

From my sister, Marg, a social worker, I learned about weekend youth retreats with kids from different schools, which expanded my circle of friends to include those from Cleveland and Lorain. We wrote letters to each other when we were separated by distance. At that time long-distance phone calls were expensive. And David was a part of this community as well. I participated in one retreat and eventually became a presenter and a leader in more weekends. It was then I started to receive the hugs I needed to bolster my self-esteem. But I was no goody two shoes either; we went to parties where we drank beer and smoked marijuana. I enjoyed all the good parts of high school except dating.

Marg had taken me on her welfare home visits when I was in elementary school where I met the mothers and kids who lived in houses different from ours – houses that were kind of smelly, shabby, and painted weird colors. She talked with them just like a friend, but I knew they were her clients. She helped them with ideas on how to do things differently. She was pretty and energetic. I looked up to her.

Marg told Mom about a program that might help me pay for college. It was called the Bureau of Vocational Rehabilitation of the State of Ohio. I went to an interview with them. I was sent to take some tests, and they reviewed my report cards. I had to go to Cleveland for one of the tests in which a physical therapist had me move my arms and legs all around. He saw that my arm was crooked but said nothing. A report was sent to the state office where I was first interviewed.

Then I was sent to another place to take tests in which I had to put little screws into holes with a timer going. I guess I was slow enough to get approved. Because of my physical problems, they determined that I would need an education in order to get work. And the education I needed was college!!! Hooray! I was approved to attend any state school I wanted in the state of Ohio, and they would pay the tuition and give $40 for books each quarter. My responsibility was to send in monthly reports and do my best. Pretty cool – finally all those broken bones paid off.

All those broken pieces inside my heart were coming together, too. Here was my silver lining. I had my eyes on Kent State.

16

Three Guys in a Volkswagen

*To be nobody else but yourself in a world
which is doing its best day and night to make you
everybody else, means to fight the hardest battle which
any human being can fight, and never stop fighting.*
e e cummings

We drove up to Bowman Hall, a four-story dormitory on the
Kent State campus. Mom parked the car in front so we could un-
load. A desk lamp, typewriter, books, and mementos all packed
in cardboard boxes had to be carried in. Judy was already there.
Her brother, Joe, helped her move in the day before. I had my
toiletries in a plastic bucket just as it was recommended. My
clothes were in my sister, Maggie's suitcase. I brought along my
Bible, my journal, and a small philodendron plant. We heard the
squeals of laughter from the girls seeing old friends again. There
was a student at the front desk, and we checked with her to get
my room key and box number for mail. Then to the elevator. Our
room number was 408. Judy and I knew each other but a third
girl, Trisha, was assigned to our room. Upon entering, I saw a
bunk bed and a separate single bed. Trisha had already moved
in and took the top bunk. Whew! I didn't want it. A huge picture
window looked out the back over the quad area. The boy's dorm
was just across the way. This adventure was going to be great! I
was full of happy anticipation, anxious to meet as many people
as possible. I saw guys with long hair wearing flannel shirts and
my heart swooned.

My college years were like a circus. My emotions went up
and down like a merry-go-round, yet classes went round and
round in repeating circles. Home being only an hour away, I kept
ties with my friends there and went home whenever I could. At

Kent State I. I felt like I was a sapling being twisted in the wind, waving at every passerby, and becoming uprooted in heavy rain. I was homesick and called home a lot. In those days we were charged a fee for every long-distance call. I ate at the cafeteria and liked the food but still did not gain weight. The study part came easy for me, although I showed a distinct disadvantage with multiple-choice tests, preferring essays in which I could wax poetic.

My circle of friends changed, so much so that by March 1972, I moved out on Judy and in with a new friend. I met Laura in English class where we both enjoyed the adjunct professor from England. He had long hair and a British accent, just like the Beatles. Whatever we wrote about sex got an A. I did not have any sexual experiences to write about, but I did write about adoption versus abortion once. My sister Maggie by that time had adopted two babies from Catholic Charities, so it was a subject I knew something about. I ended the year with a 3.5 grade average, so I was doing well, but I was sad because I did not have someone to love, a boyfriend. It was an emotional time.

I wasn't sure I wanted to go back to Kent after my first year. I began feeling less connected spiritually as well. The prayer group I had joined at the Catholic Center at school had begun to talk more about demons and spiritual warfare. This did not fit me at all, so I took a break from attending Catholic Mass. In Elyria, my mom took in young women who were pregnant and alone, so I thought I could help her there and work in her store, The Search.

It was 1973. The Vietnam War was the subject of evening news. My long hair and patched blue jeans gave onlookers no pause. We all dressed that way. It was our uniform. I had completed one year of college with no plan to return. I was restless. My prayers for guidance included prayers for an end to the war, peace for the people over there, and my selfish desire for a real boyfriend. Sure, I had friends who were guys – great friends, but none of them were trying to kiss me or anything. Was it bad breath? Did I talk too much? Was it me? I really didn't get it.

I could laugh and joke, I wasn't bad-looking. I smoked a little marijuana, but things were not going in my direction. What to do? Go West.

Talking with friends, I learned Dennis wanted to go to Colorado to attend an automotive repair school. We knew two others, Ray and J.P. who were free to travel. Nights of stoned discussion on the subject led to making a plan. It wasn't a complete plan but one we presented to our parents: we'd like to drive out to Colorado from Ohio to take Dennis to school. He had a VW bug, and we had the time. What was my mom thinking?! She gave me the go-ahead to travel over a thousand miles with three guys. I was eighteen years old.

Oh, yeah, there was a doctor in Denver who knew something about my bone condition. I could see him. Find out something, maybe, I didn't know. I had no appointment, just a name and address. That became my destination. And along the way, maybe we could get some Coors beer.

The four of us prepared. We got maps. We pooled our money. We had our Good News Bibles. Did I say I knew these guys from youth retreats? They were good guys. I packed my blue bandana and hairbrush, toothbrush and shorts. It was June 10th when we left. Written on the side of the beige bug – DENVER OR BUST. The radio blared Led Zeppelin and we sang along, all the words to "Stairway to Heaven." Then we moved on to the Beatles and the Doobie Brothers' "Jesus is Just Alright."

Our first stop was Champaign, Illinois where Dennis had an aunt. He hadn't told his mom there was a girl, me, joining the adventure. Whoops! We told Aunt Sally I was a hitchhiker. I played along. We spent the night. I can't even remember the sleeping arrangements but at that time in my life, I could sleep anywhere. I helped with supper dishes and played with Dennis' young cousin, pretending I didn't know the guys. It felt like family. Ray and J.P. were polite house guests.

Ray was the oldest of our traveling troupe. He was over 21

years old but quiet and shy. I think he had a job in a store some-where in Lorain. He had a big chest and thinning hair. He didn't have a girlfriend. J.P. was the youngest. I think he was still in high school. He came from a good family in Elyria. His name was really Jean Pierre but very few people knew that. He was just J.P. He could get wound up and excited about things. He was always nice to me, carrying my stuff and opening doors. I think he had a teeny crush on me but kept himself in check. Dennis was the looker. He had long, curly blonde hair and blue eyes. He had a lean and mean body, too. I had a teeny crush on him – that smile could slay you. We were just a motley crew of clean kids looking for adventure.

We said goodbye to Aunt Sally and hit the road early the next morning. We headed for Interstate 70 across the plains of our country. The car windows were open, and we settled in for the long ride. Trucks passed us. We tuned into a station in Kansas that played rock and roll. We snapped a few pictures of the vast sunflower fields with not a care in the world. America is wide and Kansas is flat and full of farms. My mind was in the present. I took it all in. I loved being on the road. I felt like I was Janis Joplin with Bobby McGee.

On that bright, sunny day we all started to sing "Hey! Jude" along with the radio. The car started to cough a little. We lost speed. Dennis played with the choke, but our little bug was struggling. We coasted to a stop. Dennis was able to get the car off the Interstate to a parking lot.

"What now?"

Dennis looked at the engine in the back. He had not been to automotive school yet and was clueless. We sat there fuming. We vowed to never sing "Hey! Jude" again. There was no one around for miles. We didn't know exactly where we were. We tried to find a local radio station. Everyone was tired. We ate the food Aunt Sally gave us. We slept. During the night, it start-ed to rain. The radio said something about tornado warnings. I thought of Dorothy in *The Wizard of Oz*. We were just a little depressed. I noticed a pay phone and called my mom. I told her the car broke down and she said, "Car trouble only makes for more adventure!" I had a cool mom. She said she'd call around and see who she could find to get me home.

But I didn't want to go home. The next morning was sunny and warm. There was no fixing the car. We kicked it goodbye and took our things. We decided to split up to hitchhike to Denver, Ray and J.P., and me and Dennis. I was glad to have Dennis to myself. We stuck out our thumbs. This wasn't my first time to hitch. I had hitch-hiked around the Kent State campus before. I thought we looked harmless up against the background of all those cornfields. We got rides. I felt safe with Dennis. We agreed to meet up at the Denver airport.

In my mind, this was a grand adventure. There was no fear. We even kept a travel journal. Colorado looked just like Kansas on the eastern edge. Flat. Where were the mountains? Going to Colorado was everyone's dream escape and we were there! A few more rides and we saw the mountains ahead. We were soon in downtown Denver. One of our rides was in an orange Porsche. I was a little tired, but thrilled, nevertheless.

Mom had given me a phone number for my sister's husband's sister. Dorothy was a flight attendant. I remember going to her apartment alone. She was no help. She didn't have a car for us. From her place, I found the doctor's address and she took me there. I remember sitting at a desk with the doctor and asking him if he was involved in research about Osteogenesis Imperfecta. He didn't want my blood or anything. He was a dead end.

My big plans to be a star in Denver dwindled to a tiny comet with no place to go. I was hungry, too. Dejected, I found a bus to the airport. I must have looked strange among the commuters who were dressed in style on the bus. Stapleton Airport was the only sight I'd see. Somehow the four of us found each other. We got some food. We looked around. Nobody was talking much. It became nighttime. In his wanderings, J.P. found an observation deck and a chapel. There was room on the observation deck to sleep on the floor in between the seats. We stretched out. I shared a pillow with Dennis. This was the MOST ROMANTIC moment I had ever had. We collapsed, head-to-head under the seats, while planes stopped flying and night overcame the airport.

I don't remember how the boys got home. I don't know if Dennis ever attended school in Denver. But my cool mom came through with the name and phone number of a guy driving to Ohio. He was a friend of someone she worked with. His name was Tim MacDonald, and he was driving from California. He was glad to stop by the airport to pick me up. I tumbled into the car and fell asleep. Next stop – home.

What did I learn? That God doesn't answer prayers in the manner we expect. I still had no boyfriend. The Vietnam War was not over. Going west doesn't give one new direction.

Perhaps my mother's prayer was answered. I was home in one piece.

17

Kent State - After the Shooting

After the Colorado trip I reconnected with my friend, Laura, from college. Laura lived in Oberlin, just nine miles away, so we did things together, expanding our friendship during the summer. She eventually talked me into going back to school. She was a premed student, and motivated to become a veterinarian someday. We decided to live in the international dorm for our sophomore year. We thought the international students needed to know some Americans. I walked into my room that September to find a Bible written in a foreign language on the dresser. *Oh my! Who is this new roommate?* The dorm was also co-ed, but I was sure it would not be a guy.

"Hello!" In walked the most beautiful woman with long dark hair and brown skin I had ever seen. It was Kausalya Samuel.

"Where are you from?" I asked.

"South India," she answered, and added, "My father is a bishop there. I'm here to study library science. Call me, "Kausie - sounds like cozy."

Well, this could be fun. The dorm was not crowded, so many students who had requested private rooms got them. Sometimes foreign students did not show up, so there were extra rooms available. 'Kausie' as she was called, soon opted to have a private room across the hall. She was a graduate student, and I was a mere sophomore. Although we parted as roommates, we became close friends, and remain so even to this day. In my senior year, she showed up again, looking for a place to live because of a problem with her scholarship. Laura and I, sharing an apartment by then, took her in, and she slept on a cot in our room for several months. Kausie was naïve yet poised and dignified. She had the quality of giggling and flirting with everyone, yet her knowledge of life was beyond my years. She had been an exchange student in high school in Ohio, and knew English quite well. She was learning to drive, a necessity in America. Her life in India was privileged. She grew up with servants, but her parents taught her to care for the poor and to never disrespect another human being.

The other students in our dorm were from Iran, Yugoslavia, China, Germany, Iraq, and Belgium. Laura and I became friends with many of them. The Iranians were all looking for wives, but I was not interested in them. They played ping pong relentlessly in the lounge. We were friendly to the guys, but not too friendly. I had my eye on a sharp Yugoslavian guy named Matias, but the romance was just in my imagination and did not go anywhere.

It was a wonderful time, although I did experience pain in my legs. X-rays revealed no fractures. I've learned to live with micro-fractures, not visible on x-ray. I was told to stay off my feet, got physical therapy at the student clinic, and use crutches for most of the year. The school provided transportation to class-es for a limited number of 'handicapped' students. I took advan-tage of those car rides but also hitchhiked even with crutches. I carried my books in a backpack and had access to elevators used by maintenance people. I had a sticker on my backpack that said, "I May be Slow, But I'm Ahead of You." I did not miss out on anything. I found ways to get around. I took aspirin for pain. The pain was difficult, but something I was used to overcoming.

I found my people. I was active in the anti-war movement and took classes at the Center for Peaceful Change which was created after the shootings at Kent State in 1970. I volunteered at a group home for disturbed kids. Both feet of social change were activated in me – service and action for change – even with crutches. I read about child abuse in social work class and want-ed to help kids. I traveled to various youth detention facilities to see how many kids we had locked up in Ohio. Each place was cold and isolated. The kids looked miserable, and the smell of the place was antiseptic. On one level I thought I might be an in-dividual counselor, yet on the other hand, I wanted to change the circumstances, poverty, child abuse and neglect, and the criminal justice system that made these institutions so full.

I longed to work with the poor and read the autobiography of Dorothy Day, *The Long Loneliness*. She was a Catholic activist in New York City. I also read the writings of Thomas Merton, a Trappist monk who wrote about contemplation, spirituality outside the priesthood, and social justice. His book, *Conjectures of a Guilty Bystander*, encouraged Christians to question the authorities and to live a life of simplicity. His writings resonated with me as I was trying to figure out what to do with my life.

My major was sociology with an emphasis on criminal justice. I knew a little about delinquency because of my mother's work, so I thought I might fit into that system somehow and advocate to change it after graduation. I took the opportunity to work and live at the Ohio Reformatory for Women (ORW) in Marysville, Ohio, between my junior and senior years. I wrangled a paid internship there, money that was available from a Law Enforcement grant.

Although I was committed, living at the Marysville prison was isolating. While my friends were working jobs and going out at night, I was out of sight, living on the grounds of a prison. I lived in one of the prison buildings, a room just down the hall from the inmates, only separated by a locked gate. I was not locked in. I went through a Corrections Officer's orientation for six weeks. I stayed there for eight weeks, without a car of my own to get away. For the last two weeks I worked with the prison psychologist, writing up charts on two new inmates.

The land around the prison was a working farm. The women did not work the farm, but local farmers tilled the land and spread manure and stinky fertilizer over the fields. I burned incense in my room to cover the putrid smell. Of course, this was a big hit with the prisoners down the hall. There were strict rules about exchanging gifts with prisoners. That summer one of the popular songs was, *"I Shot the Sheriff"* by Derek and the Dominos. The women sang it loudly as they walked up and down the hallway.

My best friends at ORW were those with life sentences. Most of the lifers were there because they killed their husbands. Some had already been imprisoned for ten years and were honor prisoners. They endured this regimented life with dignity. In the evenings, I attended AA meetings, chapel meetings, and other educational activities with them. We shared our life in that limited way. I was free, I would be getting back to college in September, but they were there for life, just taking one day at a time. My heart softened even more. Yes, there were some hardened criminal types there too, but I steered away from them. All in all, most of the women were mothers. The population at that time was about three hundred. Of the three hundred women locked up, over 1,000 children were separated from them. Visiting days were busy and bittersweet.

When it was time to leave, I asked to stay connected with June, my favorite lifer, but she declined saying, "You know what my life is like in here. What is there to say?" We parted with tears. I kept their names in my heart for years and wondered how they were. About ten years later, as our culture advanced to understanding battered women syndrome, those women who murdered abusive husbands were set free by the governor of Ohio. I wondered where they were.

Before we had the internet, there wasn't a way for me to find them.

I graduated in March 1975 with a bachelor's degree in Sociology with a concentration in Corrections. I received my diploma in my bathrobe via United Parcel Service while at home in Elyria. If I wanted to 'walk' for graduation, I would have had to wait until June. I was not interested in that at all. I was home in Elyria again with no plan to do any job hunting. I thought I would seek out an intentional community where I could share my desire to change things in the world. I had heard about Findhorn in Scotland, where people lived by farming and shared their lives by eating together and caring for each other's children. There the community was composed of single people and families living in trailers and an old hotel. That appealed to me, but I was not ready to go that far away. I wanted to live in a big house with lots of people, but I thought the household needed to have a purpose. Something like caring for the intellectually challenged or women being released from prison. I knew what I did not want —a job in a cubicle and car payments.

I was whole. I was able to move, work, and love. Despite my bones breaking, they also knitted themselves back together every time. I still had blue eyes and long blonde hair. I could walk and if I had an injury, the pain I had was abated by over-the-counter pain medication. In the scheme of things, my body was no worse than being obese, having epilepsy, or having diabetes. I had a crooked arm. So what?

My friend Laura and I attended a party at someone's apartment at Kent. We hardly knew the people, but we were welcomed into the typical party of flirting singles, drinking, and smoking weed. Laura and I were very much aware of social problems like poverty and racism. We did volunteer work. We kept up with the news. That week on campus there were two vastly different events. I went to hear Ralph Abernathy speak. He was Martin Luther King's successor, head of the NAACP. It was enlightening and I enjoyed it.

The other event that week at Kent State was a performance by illusionist, Yuri Gellar. He popularized the term ESP – Extra Sensory Perception. He was known for bending spoons with his mind and fixing watches. I was not impressed, so I did not go to see him.

At the party, we sat down in a circle on the floor with some other partygoers. Someone in the group started talking about Yuri Gellar. They had seen his show and were going on and on about it. They were stoned. For some reason, this raised my ire. I thought of them as simple-minded because they took this magician so seriously. I was upset because more people attended the Yuri Gellar show than attended the Abernathy speech. I had an idea. Sometimes I do not think before words come out of my mouth. It just came out. I lifted my crooked arm and said, "Yeah, Yuri Gellar, look what he did to my arm!" as I held up my crooked arm.

The cloudy-headed stoners fixed their attention on my arm. Then Laura and I promptly stood up and exited to the kitchen. There we burst into silly laughter, knowing I had blown their little minds. Yeah, it is not so bad having the affliction of *Osteogenesis Imperfecta*. Nobody is perfect.

Part Two: People Who Need People

18

Dorothy Day and The Catholic Worker

Soon after college graduation, something happened to help me to clarify what I wanted to do with my life. I met Dorothy Day, the Catholic activist. She was a kindly woman in her eighties, but her life and writing impacted people all over the world. She and Peter Maurin, a Frenchman and scholar, started the *Catholic Worker* newspaper during the depression in New York City. Besides the newspaper, they handed out coffee to folks. Over the years, it became a movement, by the same name. As I stated earlier, I had read nearly all of her books.

When David Gauchat's father died, Dorothy came to his funeral in Ohio. She was quite close to Bill and Dorothy Gauchat. I had heard that the Gauchat's home was somehow associated with the Catholic Worker, but I really didn't know the whole history. I attended the funeral Mass at St. Mary Church in Avon, Ohio, just ten miles from Elyria. Because of my friendship with David, I went to the Gauchat house after the Mass. I ambled into the kitchen to have some tea and there was Dorothy Day having coffee with Mrs. Gauchat. I sat down and they welcomed me into the conversation. Dorothy has the warmth to speak to anyone, rich or poor, young or old. She asked me what I was doing with my life. I told her I was looking for a place to be and that I wanted to work with the poor. She said, "Then come to the Worker. We can use you."

I responded with, "Okay, I'll think about it."

We continued to talk about what she was reading and what operas she listened to on the radio. No flashes of lightning, no bird landing on my shoulder, but an invitation from one of my heroes to work at the New York Catholic Worker House! This was an offer I didn't want to refuse.

At the same time, I became interested in monastic prayer. The tradition started in the third century, and continues in some forms today. Besides silent prayer, the monks also pray the *Liturgy of the Hours.* Monks work with their hands and pause seven times a day to pray. Much of their formal prayer is from the Psalms. I began to pray some of the *Liturgy of the Hours* in the morning. Later, I discovered Dorothy Day also prayed with the Psalms. She is quoted as saying, "My strength returns to me with my cup of coffee and the reading of the Psalms."

Before I made any decisions, I attended a weekend retreat to learn *Centering Prayer or Prayer of the Quiet.* Like transcendental meditation, we were taught to use a holy word or phrase and keep silent for about twenty minutes. The holy word or phrase is repeated when you find your mind wandering. I said my word to myself silently which helped me to center back into empty silence. Although I say empty, it is not truly empty but filled with the presence of God. Since then, many studies have been done to unpack all the physical, emotional and spiritual benefits from this practice. It is a practice that has stayed with me most of my life. I love this quote from Cynthia Bourgeault:

> *What goes on in those silent depths during the time of Centering Prayer is no one's business, not even your own; it is between your innermost being and God; that place where St. Augustine once said, "God is closer to your soul than you are to yourself." Your own subjective experience of the prayer may be that nothing happened – except for the more-or-less continuous motion of letting go of thoughts. But the depths of your being, in fact, plenty has been going on, and things are quietly but firmly being rearranged. That interior awakening – is the real business of Centering Prayer.*

Within a month, I started to make plans to go to work at the Catholic Worker in New York City. My work would involve

providing food, clothing, and hospitality to the poor and homeless there. I couldn't wait!

19

Soup Line

All I want to bring out is how a pebble cast into a pond causes ripples that spread in all directions. Each one of our thoughts, words and deeds is like that.
— Dorothy Day

We planned our arrival in New York City around ten in the morning. My friends, David, Greg, and Tom drove the van. It was June 1975, and I came to live and work at the Catholic Worker. We found a garage to put the van in for a few days. My friends brought me there from Ohio. Beautiful, green, and fresh Ohio. They stay a day or two, and then I will be on my own in New York City. As my friends and I walked down the street, we picked up nasty smells. We heard there was a garbage strike. On the sidewalk, when you walk over a grate, warm air blows up making it even hotter. The sidewalk was steaming, my feet sweating. I have been invited to work with the poor here. My heart is all in, yet my mind is full of questions. *Will I be accepted? Will I meet other young people besides needy people? Will I be able to keep up my prayer discipline? How will I know if this is where I'll stay for the rest of my life?*

We arrived at 36 East First Street in Manhattan with the sun in our eyes. Although there is not a cloud in the sky, this street feels gray. The buildings are old with boarded windows as if they've been in a fight; black eyes of the city; the Bowery and the lower East Side. This area is home to families who live from day to day on what they can earn and find for free. And lots of single men, shuffling along, no one making eye contact. I hear Spanish voices, Italian accents, curse words, and cars bumping along on pitted streets. We knock on the door.

Jane answered. "Hello, welcome! We've just finished the

morning soup line. We're almost done cleaning up. Come in!"

We entered the place one by one through the heavy door, finding inside a desk with an array of objects: radios, stereos, speakers, and wires. Jane offers to show us around and says, showing the table full of electronics, "That's Jimmy's stuff. He likes to fiddle with electrical things."

"This is where we serve the food." Just two long tables with chairs along both sides. In the back of the room, a kitchen with a stainless-steel island, pots hanging overhead and on a shelf above the stove. Behind the island are two industrial-sized gas stoves. Along the side of the room are three big utility sinks. We were introduced to Floyd, hard at work washing dishes by hand. He has long floppy hair and a tanned face. His arms and legs are muscular, and he looks rough, as though he has been in the sun a great deal, making his skin leathery. He smiles easily and shakes our hands. He has a raspy smoker's voice and bright blue eyes.

Jane told us they served about eighty people this morning. The heat of the summer cuts down on the numbers because even the homeless don't want hot soup on a sweltering day. Another worker comes in and jokes, "Yeah, we were thinking of changing it to a Jell-O line. We'll have forty regulars here for the evening meal. I'm cooking today," she adds.

I pick up on the leftover smell of the soup still on the stove. Out the back door is a garden area of sorts. It is a place to grab some fresh air away from the street. Plants grow along the walls crawling up the bricks and a bench. I see the ginkgo tree Dorothy Day wrote about; one of only a few trees that will grow in the city's harsh environment. Jane offered to show us the rest of the tenement. It is five stories. We followed her to the stairway back where we entered the front door.

On the second floor, they work on the newspaper, *The Catholic Worker*. We entered a large room. The green walls show wear and tear with peeling paint, showing yellow beneath. A mound of newspapers on the desk, I was glad the kitchen was cleaner. We met the men bent over tables, placing address labels on the paper for mailing. Large windows facing the street bring in the sunshine outside. It is an eight-page paper distributed by mail eight times a year. Mailbags full, these are issues ready to take to the post office. Jane announces to the guys, "This is Mary. She's come from Ohio to work with us." My friends Tom and David introduced themselves.

"Welcome," one of them says. I noticed a sign on the wall saying, "All the fits that's news to print," a parody of the New York Times slogan "All the news that's fit to print." "Let me show you where you'll be sleeping, Mary," Jane remarked.

My friends stayed on the second floor with the old men working, while I followed Jane up one more flight. This is the women's floor. In the room are five beds. A younger woman is arranging things on her bed. An older woman lies in hers. There is a small kitchen. Then Jane directed me to a bed along the wall that is empty. She said, "This one's for you." Later, I lugged my suitcase of pretty clothes up to this bed. There is no dresser. I will be living out of my suitcase. I have brought the wrong clothes. I'm a naive college graduate from a simpler place. I get the feeling I'm in over my head.

"Tonight, you can sleep in Miss Day's room," Jane offers. She must have seen the look of panic on my face. She unlocks a door at the back. Inside this room is a single bed with a pillow and bedspread. The room has a warm charm to it, with pictures on the walls, a bedside table, and a whole wall of books. "Dorothy stays here when she is in the city. Right now, she's at the farm in Tivoli." I'm happy for some privacy. Out the window, I see the hardy ginkgo tree.

Jane continues, "Above this floor are the men's sleeping quarters. The fifth floor is mostly storage."

On the roof, things seem less dull and more workable and I think of the James Taylor song, "Up on the Roof." There is a breeze and room to walk around again. Someone is trying to grow tomato plants up there. A few unmatched chairs beg us to sit down and take it all in. It seems to be a little respite from the closeness of living in a community of homeless, hopeless people. I can breathe again. Below me are other rooftops, buildings, the noise of traffic, and blaring Latino music. But at this distance from the street, my worries about spending my life here dissipate. *I'm here to be of service to the poor and needy. I shouldn't expect it to be easy. I can do this.*

What got me to this place? Since my teen years, I had known kids who had it rough. They were in the group homes associated with my mom's store. There was Chico, who had scars on his teenage face and had been in nine foster homes. When he signed his name, he added the last name of each foster family he had ever lived with. There was Tommy Zook, a Greek kid with an Afro. He stole my heart. His smile made me melt when I was seventeen. And there was Angie and her sister Rosemary. Angie and her four siblings were removed from their mother's care for some unknown reason. Angie lived with us for a couple of years. She played her records on the portable stereo and danced in a way that looked like a shuffling old man. She was so alone, not sociable, rarely made eye contact, and had trouble reading. Her sister Rosemary was developmentally delayed and lived in an institution in Cleveland. We brought her to our house for Christmas and Easter.

At Kent State, I learned more about the poor in sociology classes. Upper-class, middle class, and lower class, Americans fell into categories. I learned about the poverty index and how poverty and illiteracy can exist alongside the middle class in our society. Bargain stores sold fashionable clothes so that the less fortunate could blend in, and restaurants had pictures on the menus so that those who couldn't read could order. There were lots of ways to 'pass.' You never really knew someone until you saw their home, or in these kids' cases, the two plastic garbage bags that contained all their earthly possessions. I had visited Chico in jail more than once. Angie got pregnant as soon as she moved out of our house and back to Cleveland. Nobody knows where Zook is.

I also knew what I didn't want. Yes, I had a degree, but I didn't want to work in an office nine-to-five. I didn't want a 'real' job. I didn't have loans to pay off. I wasn't interested in having a nice car or furniture and dishes for God's sake. I didn't want a mortgage or to pay rent for that matter. I had nine nieces and nephews who were cute, but I was not in a hurry to become a mother. I graduated from college as a virgin. I had many male friends but none of the romantic sort. I was free. I wanted to be of service to others, simple as that — whatever it took, wherever it took me. I was ready, or so I thought, to work on a soup line in New York City. My motto from a Nikos Kazantzakis book was, "I have nothing, I want nothing, I am free."

I read the writings of Dorothy Day and after meeting her and decided to work with the poor at this Catholic Worker House, 36 E. First St., in New York City. She inspired me to "downward mobility." Because of conversations with her, I decided to read more, particularly Russian novels and classic literature like Jane Eyre. I also read The Prophets by Abraham Heschel around then. She inspired me when she wrote:

> *"The only way to live in any true security*
> *is to live close to the bottom*
> *that when you fall you do not have far to drop,*
> *you do not have that much to lose."*
> — Dorothy Day

Practically speaking, I had a small savings account, and I could always go back to my mother's house in Elyria to regroup. Mom loved having me home and we shared similar values. Live simply so that others may simply live. So, this is where I found myself, in a tenement in New York City, preparing to serve those on the bottom step of our society's ladder. I dove into an area I knew nothing about, homelessness in an urban setting. I was just naïve enough to think I could make a difference.

For the first week in New York City, I stayed with the women on the third floor. It was difficult having never slept in a homeless shelter before. No air conditioning. Tobacco smoke filled the room. An Italian woman had a skin condition and kept rubbing her face with cucumbers. Another woman had ulcers on her legs and spent the night changing her bandages. This was home to six women. The first night in Miss Day's room, I heard a mouse. A week later I was able to move down the street to an apartment owned by the Worker.

Throughout the summer, I visited the homes of hoarders and cat lovers. I met former actors and a UPS driver down on their luck. Lucy, a former concert pianist, asked me to come to her apartment to help her clean up. It was a small walk-up of three rooms. In the middle of the largest room, I saw cats in cages three cages high. The smell was acrid, unpleasant. I didn't help much with the cleaning since there were so many cats, it was impossible to move around. But Lucy loved each one of the cats. I think she appreciated my company.

Many who came for help had mental illnesses and no family support. There were several other new volunteers as well. I signed up to cook evening meals two nights a week for the sixty 'community' members, those who lived at the house or nearby. The soup for the soup line was prepared by more experienced volunteers. We sorted through donated vegetables on the back porch: zucchini, spinach, and squash. I had never cooked for more than two before. I just jumped right in, and the results were so-so. Yes, beggars can be choosy.

So, here I was at my first job since college graduation. I found I was not cut out for urban living. I was on my feet a great deal, and my leg began to ache so much that the pain woke me up at night. I went to the Emergency Room of Bellevue Hospital for an x-ray. Several NYC firefighters were rushed in at the same time, injured in a fire, so I never saw a doctor. They said I was fine and told me to leave. Two days later, I got a letter in the mail saying I had a hairline fracture of my tibia. I worked as long as I could, but by September I went back to Ohio to figure out another plan.

My hope to stay at the Worker for the 'rest of my life,' was not realized. I survived a summer in New York City on my own but in a community of like-minded friends. I learned I could be present to folks and not try to fix them. Lucy responded to my attention by sharing her hopes and dreams with me. She eventually moved with seventeen cats to Maine. We kept up correspondence for a few years. Rosita and her family had an apartment on Avenue "A." They came to eat at the Worker to supplement their food budget. And Mark just wanted someone to listen to him. There was little I could do to change their lives; but the Worker provided them with a place to belong.

I saw a small microcosm of anarchism: no government funds, no written rule of life, just personal responsibility. I met intellectuals who could analyze current affairs in their studied understanding of history. These lifetime Catholic Workers, the volunteers, were no-nonsense. If anything, they needed to lighten up. I'm not saying there was no joy in their shared lives, but it was, at that time, a serious crowd. They read history and politics. They knew literature and theater. But they didn't know pop songs or what was popular on TV. I guess the proximity to the down-and-out distanced them from popular culture.

I needed to go back home to rest my bones. My mind was tired, too. I knew something else would come on my horizon. To keep my hands busy while I rested my leg, I started to make a patchwork quilt for the first time.

Were my initial questions about working at the Catholic Worker answered? Yes, I was accepted. Yes, I met good people and some characters as well. My prayer life was solid. I enjoyed the prayer together in the community – the evening prayer we read from the *Liturgy of the Hours*. Would I stay at the CW for the rest of my life? Obviously not. My body was just not strong enough to live in New York City with all its walking.

20

Broken People, Pilgrimage to Rome

Humankind has not woven the web of life
We are but one thread within
whatever we do to the web,
we do to ourselves.
All things are bound together
All things connect.
Chief Seattle

I never thought of myself as disabled. Remember how upset I was when my mother asked if I wanted to go to a crippled children's camp? I hadn't had a serious fracture in years, so I was feeling more confident in my body. As I visited Our Lady of the Wayside in Avon, Ohio, more frequently, I began to appreciate, enjoy, and love the children who lived there. Some had Down's syndrome, like Suzie, who could carry on a light conversation and laughed frequently. There were three brothers afflicted with a difficult handicap, the Lech-Nyan Syndrome or uric acid syndrome. They were wheelchair bound and their hands had to be tied because if loose, their hands would fly to their eyes and poke them. Their mother had died, and their father had tried to keep the family together, but in time all three boys ended up in three different facilities. After one of the brothers moved to the Wayside, Mrs. Gauchat found the other two and took them in, too. These school-aged boys were high maintenance, but the staff assigned to them always connected with them intimately. Their intense blue eyes and dark eyelashes drew you in. And they could talk a bit, showing their intellect. But their life expectancy was short.

Volunteers and staff alike warmed to them. Although there were over twenty residents, the children and staff were one big happy family in this residential home. Even though I wasn't on the staff, I knew everyone and could interact with the children as a friend. It made me feel good and part of something good. David left to teach skiing in Colorado, but Todd and I had a very close relationship. I always made sure I had a car with a large trunk so I could throw his wheelchair in the back and take him to parties and other adventures.

All the children wore nice clothes and had decorated bedrooms. Birthdays were celebrated with balloons, cakes, and parties. At these events, I sat with Nina, the only other person I knew with *Osteogenesis Imperfecta*. I had questions for her, and she had questions for me.

"Have you ever seen your bones under X-ray?" I asked once.

"No, what do you mean?" she inquired.

"Well, when a bone is broken, you go to the Emergency Room and get an x-ray. Sometimes, the Doctor will show you the picture or you can see it up on the wall of the cast room." I answered.

"What's a cast room?"

"It's where they put plaster casts on your arm or leg, whatever is broken, so it can heal. I've had lots of casts." I continued.

But Nina had a different type of OI than I did. She was very small and had never walked. Her bones were crooked like mine from fractures. I began to understand that they didn't put casts on her breaks. Both of her legs and arms were curved. She was only about two and a half feet tall and confined to a wheelchair. My heart went out to her because her life was very limited, while mine wasn't. Her brother lived at The Wayside, too. He had cerebral palsy. They could have been cared for at home, but their parents were not equipped emotionally to parent them. Mrs. Gauchat was her mom. It was a loss she never spoke about. I tried to be a mentor for her, to give her hope. She was ten while I was twenty-one and on top of the world.

A year after college and unemployment, I became a substitute teacher for Murray Ridge School. It was in Elyria, located in the country near the county jail. The whole student body was composed of developmentally delayed and physically handicapped children. When hired to work there, it was an advantage that I already knew many of the kids who lived at the Wayside who attended there.

But I was grossly unprepared to be a teacher. My first day as a substitute was a disaster. I was assigned to a classroom of middle school-aged children, about ten of them. The teacher had to be out that day for a funeral. No one told me about the kids or their disabilities. There was no teacher aide. With unearned confidence, I entered the fray. I saw the lesson plan on the desk and learned what I was supposed to do. We went over sight words like 'emergency,' 'bus stop', 'hospital,' and 'walk/don't walk.' One boy was quite verbal and aggressive. I really had to watch him. The other students told me who was blind and who was deaf. I knew no sign language. I let them write on the whiteboard and play some games. By the afternoon, I was tired, but they weren't. At one point the deaf boy bit the blind girl who cried out. I didn't know what to do! I didn't know there was a teacher call button or an emergency procedure. I was as green as Ireland. I ran out into the hallway and called for help. There was blood!

Charlie, the big aggressive boy, started getting more anxious and pushed desks. I ran back into the room to give him attention and distract him. He got himself back under control. Someone came to give first aid care to the poor girl who was bitten. But we also needed someone to deal with the perpetrator, the kid who bit her. Other teacher aides came to the room and things calmed down. I was astonished at how quickly things fell apart. Somehow, we got them all on the bus at the end of the school day. And I would go back again, with more safety plans in hand. Incidentally, I learned to say "no" to that classroom because the behaviors were just too hard for me to handle. I didn't have the training. I had a degree in sociology, not special education.

Because of Our Lady of the Wayside, I heard about a man whose life was as dedicated to the handicapped, like the Gauchat family. He was Jean Vanier*. He was a French-Canadian man who started to live with mentally handicapped people in France, taking them out of institutions. A movement developed from his example and leadership. It was called "L'Arche" or in English, "the Ark." It consisted of many group homes of people who shared their lives with the mentally disabled. Most were in France, some in Canada, but Jean knew people all over the world. I had heard him speak in Cleveland several times. In the autumn of 1975, he organized a group called "Faith and Light" to make a pilgrimage to Rome to see Pope Paul VI. Because I was part of the larger community of the Wayside, I was invited to join them. My mom signed up to go, too. She had never been to Rome.

We were a small group of kids and staff from the Wayside. We had only two in wheelchairs, Maggie B. and Todd Gauchat. We had Suzy and Harvey, who were developmentally delayed but could walk and talk. To care for these, we had about six able-bodied adults. Our group met up with dozens more in Cleveland, Ohio, and boarded the plane to Rome. The purpose of the pilgrimage was not just to see the Pope, but to expose the handicapped to the world, and the world to the needs and gifts of the handicapped. We were given a packet of information upon arrival in Rome. It contained our itinerary, a book of songs, and a pin to wear. The pin showed a boat out on the water full of people but without oars. It was to symbolize how the handicapped must make it in the world but without all the necessary equipment.

It was a majestic experience. Jean Vanier and his people had planned activities for several days in Rome. There were tours to Assisi, Italy, and the Tivoli Gardens. It was challenging for the guys pushing wheelchairs up and down hills and steps. David almost dumped his brother, Todd in Trevi Fountain. We had several Catholic services at the Vatican just for us. One evening, we marched with thousands of handicapped people, many in wheel-chairs, into St. Peter's Basilica singing, "When the Saints Come Marching in" for a mass with Pope Paul VI. There were tears in our eyes; people of different abilities, languages, and colors, all proceeding as one.

It was for me an experience of Christian unity I will never forget.

Notes

*Jean Vanier who died in 2019, was found to have sexually abused at least 25 women who came forward to an international commission in 2020, while in the position of their spiritual director. To me he was a leader and his compassion for the disabled was inspiring.

21

From Elyria to the Apple Orchard

I was conflicted. I wanted to live my value of simplicity, serve others and go against the status quo. As the poet Rilke stated, "I don't want to be folded anywhere." But where to work? I was back in Elyria at my mom's house. She was a licensed foster parent with one teenaged girl, Kim, 15 years old, hyperactive and a smoker. We had fun times together listening to music sitting on the porch, putting together meals. As I stated I didn't want a normal job. But the state agency that paid for my college came after me. A vocational counselor called and stated I need to set up job preparation classes.

"What?"

"The whole purpose of your free ride to Kent State was to lead to paid employment," she said over the phone.

"Really?" I was flabbergasted. I set up an appointment for job readiness training. Since I didn't have my own car yet, she said they could provide transportation. The day of the appointment, a small van pulled up in front of the house. *Oh my God! They picked me up in the little bus!*

I was embarrassed big time. It was one of those vans for handicapped people and I didn't think I fit into that category. I was afraid the neighbors would see me getting in the van and believe something that was untrue about me. I was an independent woman, not a disabled woman. But I got on the bus.

At the office, the counselor was to help me prepare a resume and practice interview skills. I cooperated. I saw a job opening at Oberlin College, as a dormitory assistant. It didn't pay much, but with housing and food provided, I thought it would be neat to be back on a college campus. A mock interview was set up and it was videotaped for me to see myself in action. After seeing the video, I went home depressed. It's very hard to see yourself on video for the first time. I thought I looked like a skinny pencil, not a woman, wearing a silly smile. I laid on the couch and thought, *why would anyone want to be my friend.? I'm a freak!*

Somehow, I got out of bed the next morning and set up a real job interview at Oberlin College. The first interview with administrators went okay, but then they invited me back to eat dinner at the dining hall with the students. The Oberlin College Music Conservatory is second only to Julliard, they say. The students there are generally from the Northeast and very bright. I remember the meal, baked chicken, vegetables and rice. I pushed the carrots and peas nervously around the plate and didn't keep up with the conversation. I was out of my depth and even though I had lived in New York City, the students there didn't really care about social justice as I did. I wondered if they noticed my crooked arm as I cut the chicken. No one asked about it. I probably came across as weak and uninteresting. That old conflict surfaced "Town vs. Gown" (those who live locally in a college town versus those who attend a university). A Pollyanna. Suffice it to say, I didn't get the job. I kept looking, but opportunities were scarce.

My Mom's boss, Tom Peters, who ran Betterway, Inc. knew of my plight. By now the organization had three group homes and an alternative school. My Mom managed their bookstore. Tom arranged a job for me as a residential counselor at the Search Girls' Group Home, just a block from my home. I could walk to work. The hours were awful. When others my age were getting off work on a Friday night, I was going in. I worked all through the weekend, and most evenings. Only a few times did I have to stay overnight.

How can I describe delinquent girls, committed by the State of Ohio for breaking the law? Each was different, but their stories were much the same. Commonly the girls were raised by a single parent, poor and unsupervised with no interest in their education. Shy at first, Alice had long dark hair and a raucous laugh. She was quick to point out any injustice on the chore chart. She had been arrested for stealing a car. She had a history of running away from home. I don't remember any family members contacting the home to see her. Most of these girls had burned their bridges to family. Or the family couldn't get to Elyria to see them easily. Our job was to keep them safe, teach better decision-making, and learn to live together as long as the state sentence dictated. This was the kind of place where the aspirin had to be locked up, as well as the car keys. Radios played in every bedroom at night and most slept with the lights on.

I'll never forget my first night of work. My job was to drive the van and take the girls to the Roller Rink. Because my legs weren't strong, I didn't don any skates but sat in the gallery and watched the girls go round and round. It was boring, yet vigilance was necessary because these girls were savvy. Who knows what trashy people they might meet. If I had six girls in the van, you'd better believe I needed to return with six. I was a glorified babysitter with a college degree.

There were group meetings and conflicts mediated with common sense. Any violent behavior was punished with detention. This was not the type of 'community' I had in mind. I was 22 years old, and they were 16 and 17. They knew more about the world than I did. They listened to Black Sabbath and the Eagles, while I preferred James Taylor and Judy Collins. We just didn't jive. By the end of the summer, I was having nightmares about the girls torturing me. But I got a paycheck, and after I worked ninety days, the Voc Rehab agency closed my case.

I wanted something else. My friends, Cindy, from Washington state, and Molly, from Virginia, had been working at the group homes as long-term volunteers for over a year in 1976. Cindy invited Molly and me to Washington state to pick apples. She had a contact at a small orchard. I wasn't going to let my bones hold me back, felt healthy enough to go for it and did. I quit my first job and headed out on the road to be a vagabond.

Picking apples in Washington was where I started.

I took Amtrak across America from Elyria, Ohio to Spokane, Washington. From there, it was a bus ride to Tonasket, Washington. I was elated. I always had a notebook to keep track of my adventures. I talked to kind senior citizens on the train, played games with small children and generally made my way back and forth from car to car, a caravan of folks going West. After a long time of traveling, I really wanted to take a shower. I had walked through all the train cars by then, and figured out where the staff took showers. Picking out a change of clothes from my duffle bag, I walked nonchalantly into the staff quarters. Quickly, as the train crossed Montana swaying and bumping along, I washed my hair and body with the same bar of soap, rinsed off, dressed, and got back to my seat.

In Tonasket, Washington, Cindy, Molly, and I stayed with a family in their pickers' cabin. The old orchard's owner, Steve Kinzie, was a friend of Cindy's from the Church of the Brethren. He and his wife, Marlee, had three children, a cow, and this orchard in the Okanogan region of Washington. Steve was also a musician and former professor of philosophy in Seattle. He wasn't much of an apple orchard manager. This was a small orchard, only thirty acres, or about 150 trees. Marlee worked at a local apple-packing shed. Another friend of theirs, Billy, lived with them. He was an experienced apple-picker and, with his long arms and lanky frame, could pick ten bins of apples a day. He moved through the orchard like a man on a trapeze. We got paid seven dollars a bin. I could pick two bins a day. By comparison, Cindy and Molly filled four bins a day.

Apple-picking ladders are wide at the bottom and narrow at the top, in order to fit between branches. Hauling a ten-foot ladder was too much for me, so they found me an eight-foot ladder. We strapped ourselves with canvas bags and chose our trees for the day. Apples that drop on their own or get dropped are bruised and therefore rejected. We ate a fair share of Red and Golden Delicious apples in those wonderful weeks. We also paused to talk about life with Steve.

Steve questioned, "What did you study at Kent State?"

"Sociology and criminal justice. I even lived in a prison for two months."

"So, was it rough? What did you learn?"

"I learned that the ones who were caught for theft were usually involved in drug use. They were hard-ass women. The ones who killed their husbands, lifers, were the nicest. I missed being with my friends."

"So, what kind of books do you read?"

"Right now, I'm reading *Zen and the Art of Motorcycle Maintenance*. It's cool. I'm trying to figure out just what I'm supposed to do with my life."

"And you're Catholic? Do you pray?"

"Yes. I meditate twice a day, morning and evening."

"So that's how you get out of preparing dinner! Ha!"

"But I help with clean up!" I retorted.

Making the experience even more fun, Steve, Billy, and another friend, Lance, had a band called *The Paisley Iguana*. Billy played the fiddle; Steve played the banjo and Lance added bass guitar. Many evenings we sat outside and listened to their groovy music. This area of Washington state was occupied by back-to-nature types. And all the fruit on trees, including peaches, were picked by hippies. Further South, the vegetables in California, which required stooping like lettuce, tomatoes, and greens were picked by Latino farmworkers. I was in heaven. It never rained in Eastern Washington, the temperature was moderate, and we were able to hitchhike wherever we wanted to go.

Each day we picked out our trees and we made sure we were close enough to talk to each other. One day, my ladder tipped, and I almost fell. I must have reached too far on a limb; with the bag full of apples, it was easy to get unbalanced. Being in tune with each other, Molly heard me gasp and was able to run over and catch me and the ladder before we could topple over completely. Hearts beating rapidly, Molly and I sat down to take a few deep breaths. That was close!

When we finished that orchard, we traveled to other orchards near Wenatchee, Washington. We were so happy together. Cindy's family was in Olympia, and we visited there as well. I got to see the other side of Washington, Mount Rainer in Seattle, and the Cascade Mountains.

I also got temporary work at a daycare for the children of the pickers. Kids were named "Sky,' 'Yarrow,' and 'Dharma.' It was fun for me to play with hippie children all day and get paid. It was about the same amount as working in the orchard, but a nice break. But as the season ended, everyone had to move on and go their separate ways. Molly went back to Virginia, and I found a ride to San Francisco, where I had some friends to see. All of this was my attempt at 'voluntary poverty.' I wasn't part of 'the system.' I was looking for a lifestyle, not a job. It had been years since I had broken a bone, and I was grateful.

Here I come, San Francisco!

22

Travel and Runaways

We cannot live for ourselves alone. Our lives are connected by a thousand invisible threads ...
Herman Melville

San Francisco was all I expected. I was taken by the "painted ladies," homes like iced cookies in all different colors. The Bay sparkled when it wasn't foggy, but the Golden Gate Bridge looked too orange to be romantic. I met up with friends in the Castro neighborhood who had a large place where I could rest and enjoy my freedom. I walked the streets and went into the shops, looking at the trinkets, art pieces, and the people, of course. My friend Marilyn was taking dance lessons at a studio nearby. I met her instructor, an elegant middle-aged woman who seemed to live for dance. She told us to walk with our toes hitting the ground first. What? I tried it. It was not natural at all to me as my style was to wear long dresses and lace-up boots. My purpose of walking was to be steady, hold on to the earth and not fall.

From San Francisco, I traveled by train across Utah to see David in Vail, Colorado. It was ski season, and he was working. Looking at Utah from the train, it appeared moon-like, a strange landscape. I half expected to see a spaceship land. I allowed my mind to wander. I wrote my thoughts down in my journal. *What was my purpose? What did God want of me? Would I ever be in love?*

David met my train in Glenwood Springs, Colorado. His arms opened wide for an embrace. After so many new experiences, it was great to be with an Ohio Buckeye again. He suggested we go to the hot springs.

109

"Okay. just tell me what to do."

"I believe there are separate rooms for men and for women. It's supposed to feel great and therapeutic for your bones."

We paid the fee, then went into our separate locker rooms where we were to strip and wrap a towel around our bodies. I walked gingerly into the natural cave. There were about a dozen other women seated on a shelf in the rock. Most were older women. Very little talking. It wasn't that kind of get-to-know-each-other place. I sat and closed my eyes and visualized my bones and muscles soaking in the healing vapors. We stayed there for a half hour. After a shower, we went outside to the snowy night. It was beautiful to be outside with the mountains cradling us. But we had to get to Vail before it got any later.

We hitchhiked along the highway. I felt peaceful and calm inside and safe with my tall and muscular friend. One of our rides was in a semi-truck. It was so high up! David guided me up the ladder as the seat was well over my head. We chatted with the driver, strangers together on the road. In a few hours, we were in Vail. David was used to this kind of travel. In the 70s, there were lots of us hippies on the road.

I stayed in David's apartment when he went to work and, in the evenings, we went out to fancy bars in Vail. I have always appreciated quiet times to read and write. I never felt lonely. David and I talked about the news of Our Lady of the Wayside, who was working there, and how Nina and Todd, his brother, were doing. David told me about his rich skiing clients who gave him tips like bottles of Kahlua and tins full of cookies. One of his students was a record producer who gave him free records of new artists. At the time, Dan Fogleberg's music filled the air. The most prized possession in those years was a component stereo system, even better if you had headphones.

It was getting close to the holidays of Thanksgiving and Christmas, so I felt it was time to get back to Ohio. After another long train ride through the dark Midwest, I arrived in

Elyria again, exhausted. Mom had taken in a young woman who couldn't live with her parents, Rose. She had been released from a private mental hospital at eighteen when the insurance was no longer paying, so through the grapevine, a Catholic family asked Mom to house her for a few weeks until she could live on her own.

That was the nature of our lives. People coming and going from Twelfth Street. My social life centered around Our Lady of the Wayside and the Betterway group homes. Three new Jesuit Volunteers (JVC) recently arrived to work at the Wayside. All college graduates, these volunteers came from different places to work with the handicapped children for a year. In return, Mrs. Gauchat gave them room and board. Libby was from Brooklyn, New York. When she spoke, no one could understand her at first as she spoke a mixture of Brooklynese and Italian. Margaret was from Washington State. She played guitar and laughed easily. Kathy was also fun-loving. Over the next two years, there would be volunteers from New York, Detroit, and Germany. We shared our Catholic faith, love of service, and desire for social justice.

> *"Be doers of the word and not hearers only, deluding yourselves. Religion that is pure and undefiled before God and the Father is this: to care for orphans and widows in their affliction and to keep oneself untainted by the world."* James 1: 22,27

Other volunteers worked in Cleveland with a Jesuit parish on the poor West side. Some worked in Lorain in various youth programs. Agencies who contracted with JVC got cheap labor from young people in their twenties who were dedicated to their work. We had a happy social group, including some that were local kids and all these out-of-towners. All of us doted on Todd, who had now graduated from high school. We made sure to include him with his wheelchair in concerts, walks on the pier in Lorain, and parties.

My sister, Marg, was working with a Youth Services agency and told me about their plans to open a runaway center. I met with her boss and shared with him my desire to work with teens again. I had visited a runaway shelter in Memphis, Tennessee that summer and believed I had something to offer. He hired me and we began to make plans to open the shelter in the next few months. As Margaret completed her volunteer commitment, she decided to join me at the shelter.

We helped to fix up the house located near the corner of two state highways. We came up with the name "The Junction" because of the intersection nearby and for our vision of helping parents and children make peace with one another. With other staff, we painted walls, picked out curtains, and found donated furniture. Margaret and I were hired to be the live-in counselors. The purpose of a runaway shelter is to be open 24 hours a day so that police could bring children they found on the street to us to provide some sort of safety and intervention. And, as the program grew, kids may find the place on their own, or social workers could refer them to us.

The reasons kids run away vary. Most are from dysfunctional families with family violence, alcohol addiction, drug abuse, and even physical and sexual abuse. We received some training from a psychologist on how to do some light family therapy. Our task was to take in the child, listen to them, and within a short time, call the parents to report their presence. Primarily we needed to make the kids feel safe. The counselors worked during the daytime and set up family meetings to try to come to some agreement between the parents and children. Margaret and I cooked for them and kept them occupied until it could be worked out for them to go home. Once in a while, kids couldn't go home and waited with us to get a bed in foster care. Most stayed only a few nights while others were there for over a month. In those cases, we became very close. And we even had some repeat customers.

Margaret and I were trying out more healthy ways of eating. We tried being vegetarians. We fed the kids what we ate. We were becoming known for our homemade pizza with whole wheat crusts topped with veggies. The kids went along, but it became a running joke. One boy said he'd make up with his parents in order to get home and eat hamburgers again. The house was small so we could only accommodate five kids. Our sleeping room was on the ground floor, while the kids slept upstairs. There was a great deal of activity with kids and staff coming and going. And the phone never stopped ringing.

One morning we were awakened with a call from the secretary who worked at the main Youth Services office. She asked, "Are you missing any kids?"

I said, "No, we're just waking up."

She said, "On my way to work this morning, I drove by. You might want to go outside and look up to the second floor. I think you've had an escape."

Margaret and I ran outside in our nightgowns. Hanging from the second-story window, along the longest side of the house, we saw an open window with tied-together sheets hanging from the window. Our two runaways had done it again, running away in the night from the runaway shelter! They were not locked in, but being adventurous, they did the classic sheet escape right under our noses. We laughed until we cried, hoping this wouldn't get us fired.

I ran into an old friend, Joey at a party one night. He grew up in Avon, near David, and was part of the retreat group, The Search, back when we were in high school. He called me soon after and asked if I might want to take ballroom dancing lessons with him.

"I need a partner," he admitted. Some other friends were taking lessons and he wanted to join them.

"Sure. What night?" I said.

"Tuesdays."

I talked with the scheduling person and asked for Tuesday nights off for the next few weeks. It turned into months and Joey became my first real boyfriend. We slogged through the wet winter of northern Ohio and by spring I was spending all my time off with him. He was a house painter, who still lived at his mother's house then. He later became a house flipper, before it was the trend it is now. He took an old home in Lorain, fixed it up, and then sold it. I don't know how he financed this, but he had money. He was very particular about paint color, wallpaper patterns, and his tools. Everything he owned, including his socks and radio, were splattered with paint.

We learned the waltz, the rumba, and the cha-cha. We went out on occasion to dance bars. I still didn't wear high heels for these events, but I ditched the boots. We also went to movies and dreamed of making a cross-country trip someday in his van. Marriage was not even considered. He came to my family's Christmas gathering and I was present with his family when his father died. His mother loved me, of course. I was a "good" girl and Joey could be wild. I guess he was my walk on the wild side. I knew that he and his friend, Tom, did drugs together.

I was invited to join a 'prayer group' by people I knew in Lorain. It was facilitated by an ordained Brother in the Catholic order called the Missionary Servants of the Holy Trinity. They ministered in South Lorain in the Latino community. One of their principles was to develop lay people to be missionaries as well as "in the providence of their daily life." This group called the Cenacle met every other week to discuss their daily life, their ministries, and their spiritual lives. We met at the priest's house. This Trinitarian order started in the early twentieth century by a Vincentian priest, Father Thomas Judge. It grew into an American missionary group, searching out the poor and empowering the laity to be ambassadors of Christ. The priests headed up parishes in Black, Indian, and Latino parishes in the U.S., Puerto Rico, and Mexico. Nuns who were also called Trinitarians, worked in schools and parishes with the youth. They were all progressive in their approach.

At our meetings and retreats, besides Mass and Bible study, we read the early writings of Thomas Judge. He laid out his thoughts and revelations in a book of "Conferences." Typically, someone would choose a selection from the book, and then we would discuss the ideas, relating them to our daily lives. Everyone was doing some kind of work with "the abandoned" as we called them, using Father Judge's word. I was working with troubled kids, another was doing Catholic education, retreat work, or youth work. It was a way to give support to each other. It led me on the path of much spiritual reading. And after a time, my mother joined the group as well. This group would become very important to both of us.

> *The Missionary Cenacle makes you a light in dark places. Makes you the strength of the weak, a tree under which the poor and oppressed and the hearts that are tormented may receive refreshment.*
> – Father Thomas Judge

Margaret decided to leave the Junction and headed to Alaska to be a Jesuit Volunteer again. I contacted my old college roommate. Mary Murphy and I decided to take advantage of cheap airfare and spend the summer in Europe. I resigned from my position at the runaway shelter. Mary was a teacher so had the summer off. We made our plans, got a Youth Hostel card, and found airfare to Luxembourg via Iceland for less than $200.

Off we went.

116

23

Backpacking Through Europe

Afoot and lighthearted I take to the open road,
Healthy, free, the world before me
Walt Whitman

Our summer in Europe was incredible. Mary and I traveled from country to country, using our Eurail Passes and Youth Hostel cards — Europe for less than $10 a day. We stayed overnight in Reykjavik, Iceland, with a social worker who had visited our Elyria group homes. She showed us around, and we experienced the Scandinavian summer nights wherein the sun never goes down. It was like our dusk, but never dark. Even in the house the natural hot volcanic water flowed from the pipe. However, our luggage never arrived in Iceland.

Bjorg drove us to Thingellir a national park that had been the site of the Icelandic Parliament from 930-1879. It was stark and cold but nevertheless beautiful with volcanic mountains in the distance with heather and arctic thyme at our feet. Bjorg was thrilled to show off her country.

"We have precious few trees, so we care for them to keep them alive."

Coming from Ohio I realized we took for granted our lush countryside.

"All our water comes from hot springs," she said. "If you want to take a bath at the house, there is plenty of water."

As we drove back into the city, we noticed several hot springs outside that were being enjoyed by others at ten o'clock at night, still light outside. It would have been nice to spend more time with Bjorg and her family, but we had a schedule to keep so back at her home, we slept fast and left in the morning for Luxembourg.

When we deplaned, our lost luggage was waiting for us in the Luxembourg airport. Eureka! Then we found the train station and headed to Tubingen, Germany where I knew another former group home worker, Herbert. A college student, he welcomed us to his dorm room to spend the night. On that summer night, he hosted a party in his room with music blaring, people dancing and German/English conversation until the wee hours of the morning. Herbert was studying psychology. He was a studious guy. He and his friends smoked marijuana sometimes, too. Herbert said, "I do it for the insight."

This made me smile; a serious student does not smoke weed to have fun but to learn. He took us to eat at the student cafeteria in town. They served us a large plate of meat and noodles. We walked the streets taking it all in. Both of us loved all the different sites, the church tower, the red rooftops, and the people. Ending another short visit, we headed out again by train to the Rhine River area.

We stayed in a youth hostel that was at the top of a hill. I struggled carrying my backpack and soon we found ourselves in a clean bunkhouse where we spent the night. This was the first of our hostel experiences. Most of them were filled with younger people, but we were happy to sleep somewhere safe for $8 a night. So far so good. Mary and I were getting along and laughing at everything new.

In Koln, Germany we met up with my cousin, Kathy from New York and traveled with her and her niece to Switzerland. We had a nice hike in the Black Forest before leaving Germany. On the train, somehow, we ended up in a first-class berth together, all four of us. Halfway through the night, we were awakened by the train staff who checked our tickets. Our Eurail tickets were only good for coach seating, so Mary and I picked up our belongings and found another seat. No sweat.

The four of us toured Lucerne and stayed in a real hotel. It was gorgeous, decorated with flowered bedspreads and curtains. I felt spoiled. In town, we drank beer and celebrated the Fourth of July. The best part for me was gazing at the Swiss Alps from the train, rounding corner after corner of amazing views. Mary and I watched our spending and usually ate only one meal a day. The next stop was back in Germany, in Berlin, which at the time was still a walled city. There we visited the family of Matthias Kresser, a former volunteer at Our Lady of Wayside. On Sunday we attended the Lutheran Church services with Matthias' family.

Singing along with the hymnal, Mary and I tried to pronounce the German words, broken into syllables. By the second song, we got the giggles and could not stop laughing — our shoulders wiggling up and down as we prayed Matthias' parents would not be upset with us.

Through my volunteer friends at the Wayside, I arranged to meet up with a group from L'Arche on vacation in Brittany, on the coast of France. The L'Arche members were camping out on cots in an empty old school. They found a house near the property for us to bunk in. It was one of those old servant houses for a manor. The walls were about two feet thick. It was a wonderful week in which we got to know the staff and residents, even without speaking French. We took our meals with them at the school and washed dishes as a group after dinner. We sang and prayed and just enjoyed the life of that small village in France. Another unforgettable time. The mentally handicapped can really teach us 'normal' people about joy.

The next stop was Belgium to see a college friend, Beatrice Hanoulle, at her family home. Beatrice showed us around Flanderland. The culture is similar to the Netherlands. We saw windmills and the beautiful green countryside. She also took us to some of the graveyards from the World Wars, sobering, to say the least. We went to the beach at Ostende, where odd to us, no radios were allowed. I guess the Belgians like peace and quiet at the beach. It was a long expanse of a light gray beach. After a few days, Mary began to get anxious about getting home. She decided to curtail our planned visit to England in order to catch the cheap flight to the U.S.

I stayed and continued my plan to go by ferry to England and meet up with my friend, Ann Courson, a French girl who was working at a Bed and Breakfast in Scotland. Never one to be anxious by myself, I found the train to Scotland but had to spend the night in an English town on the way. I carried my backpack and stayed in a cheap hotel, catching the train to Edenborough. I met some other American girls on the train. We shared our adventure stories and ate dinner on the train. I was impressed by the linen tablecloths. Little did I know about train dining. The tablecloths were piled one upon the other like pancakes. When we finished dinner, they removed the tablecloth and there was another clean one below.

I spent a couple of nights with Anne at the B&B. It was owned by a woman from South Africa. She had two darling daughters. We picked blueberries in the yard, while I smiled at their dainty Scottish accent. Soon it was time to move on again. Anne headed back to Paris where she lived, and I got a train to Forres, Scotland on the northwest coast. There was lots of talk about the Loch Ness monster in far north Scotland was my next destination. Findhorn is a large intentional community of like-minded, off-the-grid, kind of people. Some lived in trailers while others had rooms in the large main building, which used to be a school or the headquarters of a fancy golf course. The place had lovely grounds. I registered to spend a week there in their work/visitor program. During the mornings we had chores to do along with the community members while afternoons were spent exploring and visiting with each other. There were thirty in my group; people from all over the world. I was very comfortable there. It was the first time I had a bath in a bathtub since Iceland. My leg was aching from all the walking, so it was a welcome benefit. One of the group members was named Claire, and we hit it off like we had known each other for years. She lived in Manchester, England.

After this week, it was now September and I needed to get back to Ohio and get a job of some kind. I made my way back to

London, hitchhiking with my left thumb. There I took advantage of a cheap Freddy Laker airfare of $125 from London to New York. But to get that fare, I had to wait in line at the airport for over 24 hours. There was a tent outside set up for those in line. It was well organized; each hopeful passenger was given a folding chair in a row with six feet of space in front of the chair. Weary travelers rolled out their sleeping bags, as I did, and waited our turn. During the long wait, I wrote letters and in my journal. I was happy to have completed my journey for under $1400. I saw old friends and made new ones. I had leg pain, but no fractures.

I was ready for whatever my next chapter would bring.

24

Venezuela

Though we travel the world over
To find the beautiful,
We must carry it with us
Or we find it not.
Ralph Waldo Emerson

In order to tell the story of my life in Venezuela and my struggle to learn Spanish, I must go all the way back to high school and college.

Edilio Neyrone was an Italian missionary to the United States and a priest with a gift for calligraphy. He was assigned to teach Spanish at the Catholic high school I attended. On the first day of my freshman class in 1967, Padre Edilio told us that German was the language used to talk to dogs. *"Ach tung! Komm her!"* he said sternly in his most guttural German accent. However French was the language used to talk to the ladies. Mademoiselle, *vous etes si belles!* he said in an exaggerated French accent. But Spanish, he said, is the language used to talk to God. He closed his eyes and folded his hands as if in prayer and said the first line of *The Lord's Prayer* Father in Spanish. Oh my! He should have stuck to making art with his pen! As a teacher he was clueless.

Our class was just not that interested. It was the sixties. No one wanted to be a Spanish scholar. Our only interests were The Rolling Stones and the next football game. One day in class Padre Edilio, dressed in his long black cassock, glided up and down the rows of desks, checking our homework. Very few students had done it. By the time he reached my desk, his frustration was full-blown. I made some sort of remark under my breath, and he hauled off and whacked me with the flat of his hand on the top of my skull. "Ouch!" I stood up, gathered my things, and walked straight (without a hall pass) to the principal's office to report him. It didn't happen again. I can safely say that no one learned much Spanish that school year.

I graduated from high school in 1971 and headed off to Kent State University. To obtain a Bachelor of Arts degree, one had to meet a language requirement. Since my toe was in the water already with Spanish, I signed up for a class. I fancied myself being a social worker someday and needing Spanish fluency to talk to Latino clients. I didn't work very hard in this class either, I confess. In fact, I earned my first-ever "F" on one assignment. Rebellious and proud of my "F", I hung the paper on the refrigerator at the house I shared with six other students. I thought it was funny. I was taking the class pass/fail which meant I could pass with a "D" and it wouldn't affect my GPA. But speaking Spanish was another matter. I found out just how much I didn't know when I landed in Venezuela.

How in the world did I get there? After my adventure in Europe, I was welcomed home by Joey, and we resumed our relationship. David was back from cooking school and in the process of opening his own bakery in Cleveland. I picked up some work as a substitute teacher and tutor in public schools, but I really had no career direction.

Sister Mary Stoltz, my mother's cousin and a Maryknoll missionary, contacted me by letter from Venezuela. She knew I was not yet settled into a profession. She had met an Italian woman at the beach who was interested in having her children learn English from a native speaker. In exchange, the Italian woman, a linguist, would teach me Spanish and provide a small stipend. Would I like to come to Venezuela? I said yes, of course! I was twenty-six years old.

I obtained the necessary visa and flew south – waaay south. When I got off the plane in Venezuela, everything was dusty and brown. *Yo no sabia ni pan ni papas.* (I knew neither bread nor potatoes.) And it was a long way from Ohio's comfortable culture!

The Italian couple picked me up in an open-air Jeep at the Barcelona, Venezuela, airport. They both spoke English well, for which I was thankful. The two little Italian children smiled at me with their dark eyes and giggled. We arrived at the house and I settled in. The weather was hot and humid. I had my own room. The house was air-conditioned and there was a ceiling fan over my bed. The beach was just a short walk away. Fantastic!

Irene and Mateo were eight and five years old, respectively. Sometimes they wanted to play school and learn English. Most of the time they wanted to run around the house and have me chase them.

Each afternoon Renata, their mother, would sit down and converse with me in Spanish. She had me read the novel *From the Garden* by Jerzy Kosinski in Spanish. My vocabulary increased. It was the story of a simple gardener who worked for a millionaire. He spoke in short sentences, which made reading the book much easier for me. The gardener become famous because the millionaire interpreted his brief statements as nuggets of genius. He ultimately became a cultural icon. How ironic that I learned to speak Spanish from an Italian woman using a book penned by a Polish writer.

After about two weeks, Renata and her husband decided to move the family back to Rome, Italy. Her husband was in the plaster business and felt it was a good time to leave Venezuela. I was now out of a job and a place to live! *O Dios mio!*

Que sera' sera.' I moved across town to live with my cousin, the nun who had invited me to come to Venezuela in the first place, just until I could make other arrangements. Sister Mary, who was in her sixties, had been a missionary most of her life. Her work until this assignment had been in the business office. She was short, a bit overweight, and "efficient" — that is to say, she never really picked up on that Latino *suave*. She lived with another nun, also named Sister Mary. They shared a small cement block house in a middle-class u*rbanizacion* or housing development.

The two Sisters Mary did not get along. Sometimes we had meals together. Sometimes the front door slammed because they just could not see eye to eye. I was caught in the middle, being amiable to both. Furthermore, the arrangement was not good for my Spanish because three Americans together naturally speak English.

In Barcelona, the Catholic missionary activity was not traditional. The two nuns, a young American couple with a child, and two priests formed a team. They all lived in separate houses. They did not minister in church, hospital, or school. They lived among the people and did community organizing. Sister Mary, my cousin, had a weekly group with women, a support group or assertiveness training to empower women. I made some new friends there.

Then another opportunity came my way. A Peruvian family wanted their children to learn English, and they could provide me with a place to live. Hooray! Out of the "convent"! I moved back to my former neighborhood near the beach. With the Golz family, I shared a bedroom with their two teenage daughters. They also had a younger brother who was about twelve years old. It was a fun, busy household and the girls were polite and well-mannered. The family also had a maid, Carmen, from Lima, Peru, who was closer to my age. At times, I would invite her out for coffee. Another diversion was to attend Mass in the village of Lecheria several evenings a week around sunset at 7:00 p.m. I have no idea what the Colombian priest did all day. He was a plain-looking man about forty-five years old who wanted to practice English with me.

Padre Ray was serious at Mass but jovial afterward when he had a group of teenagers and young adults taking classes in church theology. Sometimes the group of us just spent time together and talked to him about music and culture. At times, I was afraid of walking home alone in the dark, but it was a safe village. As for my Spanish, I was getting a lot of conversational practice. I mastered the Mass prayers because of all the repetition. I guess Padre Edilio Neyrone was right: "Spanish is the language used to talk to God."

Soon I learned a new Spanish expression: *Mala de comportamiento*. It meant "bad behavior." I had offended the Golz family by having a friendship with their maid. And my behavior was suspect because I walked to Mass in the evening alone. I was asked to leave after the first month. As luck would have it, I met a blond-haired, blue-eyed Spanish woman at the post office. She invited me to go sailing with her and her husband. Of course, I went. It was a grand day on the water, gliding in the Caribbean with affable people and ham sandwiches. Maritza and I saw each other again and became friends.

Maritza was from Spain but had lived in Venezuela all her married life. Her husband was German and worked in construction in the southern part of Venezuela, in El Tigre. Together they had four children, all teenagers. Maritza's father was a famous editorial writer for the main newspaper in Caracas. One day Maritza cried to me that her father invited her to go with him back to Spain for a visit. She had not been back to her country for twenty years and was longing to go but couldn't because of the children. The two oldest were away for the summer but the two children at home, Miguel and Susy, were going to start school in a few weeks. They were fifteen and sixteen years of age, respectively. Fritz, her husband, came home infrequently, so Maritza asked if I could stay with her two kids so she could go to Spain for four weeks. I said yes.

So I moved into my fourth home in Venezuela. Things were laid back. Maritza said her husband would be home in a few weeks to give us money for groceries and gas. I had begun teaching private English lessons in the village near the beach, so I had a little money. I went to my appointments several days a week and stayed overnight with Miguel and Susy. They loved having an Anglo-looking babysitter! They spoke little English, but I managed to keep things in order at the house and cook for them. We didn't see Fritz for several weeks. I had to learn to drive their yellow Volkswagen Bug to take them to school. It was tricky to learn to drive a stick shift for the first time. Several people took me out driving. I practiced in the neighborhoods where the streets were paved but did not have traffic. The kids yelled at me to do this or that while driving the car, but I didn't even know the word for "stop!" In time, I learned and drove with confidence. I drove the two teens to their school, about ten miles away. The name of the school was "Walt Disney." I don't know if it was a public or private school, but they didn't wear uniforms.

The kids and I had a lot of fun. We went to the movies and watched the Three Stooges and Mary Tyler Moore on the television in Spanish. We dealt with limited food supplies because their dad had not come home to give us money. Once, the washing machine broke. We went to the repairman's house, a cousin of sorts, to ask him to fix it. We had running water and electricity and lived in a solid house surrounded by palm trees. Finally, Fritz came home for a couple of days. He was grouchy without Maritza to make him happy. He smoked and threw the ashes and butts on the floor. I really didn't like him. He did give us some money for food, but then he was gone. I suspected he had another woman in El Tigre where he worked.

I was able to speak good conversational Spanish after all these weeks. I would wake up and tell Susy what I dreamed about in Spanish. I enjoyed the good coffee and my freedom. For teenagers, they were well-behaved. They stayed around the house and did their schoolwork. When Maritza came home, I figured it was time for me to move on.

Sister Mary and I took a weekend trip to the Isle of Margarita just for fun. Then, before going back to the States, Sister Mary and I traveled to the western part of Venezuela. I saw Barquisimeto and Barinas, a farming area in the south. We visited missionary houses there and ended our exploration of Venezuela in Merida, high in the Andes near Columbia. There was a university there and a historic cathedral. In Merida, we wore sweaters for the first time since I landed in Venezuela.

My stay in Venezuela ending, I went back to the church to see Padre Ray and the youth group. While playing cards, I broke one of my fingers. The game was like our American card game of "spoons", but instead of grabbing a spoon when you got four of a kind, you just slapped your hand in the middle of the table. The hand on top lost. My finger got crushed in the first hand. I pretended like it was okay for a few more rounds, but when I got home, one finger was swollen and hurt badly. I spoke to my cousin about it but having no insurance or standing in the country, I wasn't sure how to get an x-ray and medical care.

Then I remembered teaching English to three daughters of a local Venezuelan pediatrician. I went to see him at home. He gave me a piece of paper and told me to take it to a clinic in Puerto la Cruz, a town nearby. The paper said, "Please treat her; she is my cousin." This is how things went there. I was privileged enough as a visiting American to know the right people. I got my x-ray and splint for my South American fracture. I left Venezuela from Caracas, the capital, and returned to Ohio after six months in South America as an English teacher.

Once again, my quest for the right situation to use my gifts and desire for adventure did not work out as planned. I returned home to regroup. My Spanish fluency was much improved, I had made some great friends, and I found out I was pretty darn adaptable. I lived with three different families in those six months. I traveled light. I loved the land and the people of Venezuela.

Yet, I hoped this time to go back to Elyria and find a full-time job.

25

Hometown Challenges

Well-meaning people would make suggestions about jobs I might apply for when I was between trips. One said I should be a highway toll collector while another suggested I could be a phlebotomist! Really?

I didn't see myself as either of those. After the Venezuelan adventure, I came back to Elyria to regroup. A friend of ours, who knew about Jean Vanier and his ministry to the mentally handicapped, was working in a newly opened group home for older men. It was just two blocks from Twelfth Street. They needed someone to work the day shift at the group home, named Cedar Place. I interviewed and got the position. Cedar Place was located next to a nursing home, in a building where the caretakers of the nursing home used to live. It had four bedrooms and could accommodate eight mentally retarded men over the age of fifty-five.

Those eight men became "my old men" in the year and a half I worked with them. All had been hidden away in the State Hospital for many years. With the move toward deinstitutionalization, a select few were moved to Elyria. My job was to get them involved in our small town, learning how to cook their own breakfasts, shave, and obtain employment at the local sheltered workshop. It was a perfect job for me. Only one had any family to speak of. Marty had a sense of humor. Jim had a heart of gold. Julius made three poached eggs each day for breakfast and don't get in his way! Gus was everyone's friend. Donald loved marching band music. The day I took them all to the Fourth of July parade, he actually wept for joy seeing and hearing the marching bands. Paul was the only one with a bad attitude. It took him six months to address me by my name. He wasn't a happy fellow. Neil smiled easily and was always a willing helper. James loved to ride his bike downtown Elyria. He never met a stranger.

One Day I took them to my uncle's dairy farm in Wellington, Ohio. They shuffled around the farm taking in the sights and smells of the country. They left with ball caps advertising corn feed and car dealerships. Back at the house, they practiced printing their names and learning their address. Everyone had a fun time, especially me. A small Faith and Light group formed in Elyria. On one evening once a month, we would gather at someone's home to have a Catholic Mass and social time with the mentally retarded adults in the community. It was modeled after the love Jean Vanier demonstrated to the L'Arche homes in France.

But after a year, my itchy feet urged me to move on. A friend was leaving her job in child welfare at the local county Children's Services agency. I arranged to get that job and resigned from Cedar Place with time to have a month of travel between jobs. I took a short trip to Virginia to see my sister, Maggie, who lived there now. And David and I traveled back to the Catholic Worker in New York City to see Dorothy Day as she was getting on in years.

At the Lorain County Children's Services, I became a protective services caseworker. That means I was assigned a dozen troubled families to monitor. These parents were deemed at risk for abusing their children. Most were single mothers supported by welfare payments. Several other families were my responsibility, too. They had their children in foster care because the situation was so dire, the children could not be left in their care. I had a wonderful supervisor, Carol, who guided me.

Within the first couple of weeks, I visited a woman in Lorain named Janet. Her diagnosis was schizophrenia. She wasn't working, and her daughter, Rose had been removed from her care because she left her alone frequently. Rose, a teenager, had begun to get into trouble with the law. I went to Janet's house and it was then I knew I had a lot to learn. I knocked on the door and after five minutes, a large woman in pink baby doll pajamas opened the door. This was Janet, the mother I was supposed to reform. I had no idea what we were supposed to be talking about. Janet had just moved into her apartment, and it looked adequate.

"Where's Rose?" she asked.

"I'll arrange a visit for you two as soon as I can," I spoke. "She's in a foster home in Elyria."

After that introduction, we talked about rent money, Rose's shot records, and getting a phone. There were always barriers for these women to overcome. Finances were dismal. Most lost their welfare checks when the children were removed. Janet had no car, no phone and could barely read and write. I came to realize the mental health diagnosis was probably wrong. She wasn't schizophrenic; she was just developmentally delayed. A neglectful mother had raised her, so she didn't know what would be best for her daughter. They were like two ships on the sea with no captain, just floating from harbor to harbor.

I worked hard, documenting everything and sometimes testifying in court. One family was referred to me because the children were showing up at school in dirty, shabby clothes and their mother didn't respond to any of the school's outreach. I went to the house several times and they would not open the door. We had phone conversations in which the mother gave excuses for every missed appointment for seeing me or getting her kids to doctor's appointments. Finally, the door opened when I brought Christmas gifts for everyone. I sat in a chair in the living room as roaches crawled on the carpet in front of me. The mom explained to me that every Saturday night they took their baby, Brian, to concerts and wrestling matches, dressed as a superhero. There he garnered the spotlight and was known as a mascot for the band and wrestlers. She was immensely proud of this while the five older children were sorely neglected. I was able to get an exterminator to the house. He reported to me it was the worst case of insect infestation he ever saw. I am not sure how much I moved the needle toward improved parenting, but I tried to show respect and kindness while encouraging change.

There were many family stories of abuse and neglect in which I tried to make a positive difference. Not all cases ended well. In one case a family of six was living in a car when the coroner contacted our agency to say a baby had starved to death. Carol and I were told the rest of the children looked bad, too. The police intervened and they were put up in a hotel for the night. We went the next morning with court papers to remove the rest of the children. Because of severely miscalculated priorities, the father insisted that when food was scarce, they fed the boys before the girls. And the father was a boxer in decent shape. He fancied himself a minister of sorts. We had the police call him to the station, while we went to the hotel. We found the two little girls near death from lack of food; one looked like the photos I had seen of the children in Biafra. The mother was also very thin. She cried out in misery as we took the children to our cars. It was devastating for me as well, hearing the cries of the mother and children. On one hand, the children needed to be safe and fed, however taking children from a scared and desperate mother will never sit well with me.

The baby named Grace was two years old and weighed fifteen pounds. Her older sister, Mercy, was eight years old and weighed just forty pounds. We took Grace to the Emergency room where I was able to give her a bottle of formula to begin the healing process. This case took all my energy and compassion for months. It was reported in the local newspapers and the parents were both arrested for child endangerment. The court case was especially emotional as I had to testify that they had no address, homeless at a time when this was not part of our everyday vocabulary. The Judge did not understand how someone could have no address. He berated me on the stand. It was 1982 when Reagan was president. Poverty was increasing because of budget cuts to welfare programs. Most of the country lived on the fabric of normalcy, while I was viewing the threads on the backside of the material, loosened threads, knots, and missed stitches. I longed for the people in Congress to care about poor and needy families.

Recently I saw a meme on social media near Halloween stating, "You Can't Scare Me, I'm a Social Worker." Our team of caseworkers supported one another in our work. We sought out training and new ways of engaging families. We became close friends. Burnout was real. After two years of this work, I decided I wanted some distance from the United States and applied to be a lay missionary in another country. I hoped for a simpler lifestyle where I could help those in a more basic way. I also wanted the spiritual support of a faith community. I applied to a lay volunteer missionary program out of New York.

26

Social Justice, Social Service

Let us remember that optimism is not essential to a spiritual person, only hope. God does not call us finally to be successful, only to be faithful, which means that when we can't be optimistic, we can still be persistent.
Rev. William Sloane Coffin, Jr.

I carefully considered which Catholic missionary group to join. I applied to Maryknoll, the same one to which my cousin, Sister Mary, belonged. Most of my friends were involved in work for change on some level. I had two new friends: Helga from Germany who came to Elyria to do community organizing with senior citizens, and Gerrit from the Netherlands who worked in the delinquency group homes. Together we clowned around on our off time, took hikes, and went into Cleveland for the Art Museum and bars. David was back now and opening his own bakery in Cleveland. Some friends were getting married, but many friends were busy with things other than building "the American dream." In fact, it never really occurred to me that I should be establishing a credit record or moving out of my mother's home. My mind was busy, busy, busy with work, work, work.

I volunteered to be a presenter of a program in the Catholic churches about the enormous spending and overkill of nuclear weapons. This work brought me in touch with other local people who cared about peace work. There were meetings to attend all over. Some were large and some small. To me, all of it was fun; I really dug in with effort when it was something I believed in. I began to meet more people with common interests. My Mom and I joined a busload of people attending a Nuclear Freeze March in New York City. When we got there, we were a quarter of a million strong. As it turns out, the United States did not get rid of one nuclear weapon, but what we accomplished was to get others to question the whole notion. And now even the Catholic bishops were on board. They published a paper on Peace and Denuclearization.

I was invited to work with the Catholic Commission on Community Action. It was a large committee of movers and shakers in the church. This taught me even more about social change. There were people organizing around redlining, a bank practice of not lending money in neighborhoods that were either poor or African American. I learned about Food Banks and food policy. The group was also looking into the employment practices of the Diocese of Cleveland. My mind was swimming with causes. *What could I do? What was MY calling?* I was twenty-nine years old.

At the same time, I was continuing to meet with a smaller Catholic group called "the Cenacle." After two years, I felt I had done enough in Child Welfare work. I was tired. I thought about returning to a Third World country, instead of sitting at meetings all the time. I wanted to get my hands dirty. I wanted to be WITH the people. I applied to become a Maryknoll Lay Missionary. This group was the crème de la crème of American lay missionaries. It was the community to which my great uncle Fred and Sister Mary Stoltz belonged. They had placements all over the world. I had to travel to New York, their headquarters, to have a psychological evaluation. The application included an essay about my motivation to do missionary work. I enjoyed putting my heart and soul on the paper. I worked on it for several weeks. I felt I had a vocation for missionary work.

After what seemed to be a long wait, I received a letter back that said I was accepted. They wanted to send me to Korea to work with Amerasian children in an orphanage. What? For some reason, I just didn't think Korea was the place for me. I was thinking I would like to go to Venezuela again, so I wrote back and turned down Korea, asking instead for a Spanish-speaking country, possibly Venezuela. Then I waited.

The child welfare agency knew I was about to leave. I had been there two full years and was ready to move on. Finally, I heard back from Maryknoll again. The Venezuelan team had reviewed my application but didn't feel they could offer me a place to work due to my medical needs. It was the bone fractures they were worried about. They didn't want to put me at any risk and the mission areas in Venezuela could not guarantee specialized medical care.

"It's just not fair," I moaned. I had the heart of a missionary but not the body.

I kept on and dried my tears. I still didn't want to go to Korea. It just didn't fit. I knew in my heart I wanted to be in the Americas.

As always, things were put in my path to show me what I needed to do. The Cenacle had a retreat in June 1983 in Cleveland. The head of the Missionary Servants Lay Volunteers, Harold Grant, was there. Outside in the glare of Cleveland's sun, I told him of my difficulties with Maryknoll. I said I felt I had something to offer, and I really wanted to serve. He said, "They may not want you, but we want you." That was it. He said I could work with their mission team in Mexico. The application was just a formality. He knew of my involvement in the Cenacle, which was their branch for the lay mission work of the Missionary Servants. He knew I was mature in my desire to help and had deep faith. He was the open door I had been praying for.

I resigned from my position and put my retirement money into a CD. I prepared to attend the week-long training session in Holy Trinity, Alabama, return home for a week, then be on my way to Mexico. I would turn thirty years old while on retreat.

The week of preparation for the mission in Alabama was perfect. The retreat center was in a rural area outside of Columbus, Georgia. It was my first trip to the Deep South. It was hot and muggy, the woods were all pine, and the kudzu was everywhere. I joined twenty-five other like-minded individuals getting ready to work in missions all over the country. I was the only one going to Mexico. We prayed and laughed together and learned more about the spirit of the Missionary Servants. This group of priests and sisters had ministered in Lorain, Ohio, with the Puerto Rican community for years. In fact, I knew many of them. Workshops were on cultural differences, liturgy planning, and community building. It was like being in a family. We were commissioned to go out into the world to share Christ's love.

My journal entry: *"Today we considered the Holy Agony of Christ. I spent some time outside with a tree and wrote down all the things that need healing within me. Then I threw the list away and went to the sacrament of reconciliation in the evening. I'm feeling less afraid of Mexico. I'm getting anxious to go. A week is long enough for me to study and pray. Now I want to work. It's time to really trust in God."*

I flew from Cleveland to Miami, changed planes, and flew to Mexico City. There the other lay volunteer, Maria, met me. Together we took a bus to Buenavista-Tomatlan, Mexico via Uruapan. As we traveled, the countryside became increasingly wild. We arrived at an underdeveloped region where my job was to help in the Catholic parish and hopefully help to put together a medical clinic. I lived with two Missionary Servant sisters: Sister Margarita and Sister Carmen Teresita, both Puerto Rican with many years of mission experience behind them. Sister Margarita previously worked in Ohio. The mission priests lived down the hill in a large Spanish-style house next to the church. They were Father Eugene and Father Jesse, a younger priest from Lorain. Father Eugene was also from Ohio. He had a German heritage, was a good leader, and was very methodical. Maria was another volunteer who had been working there for a year, which gave her some authority. She was good at bossing me around. On the day we met, to avoid confusion, she asked me to use my middle name, Monica, so there wouldn't be two Marias. I felt okay about the name change, but Maria and I never became close friends.

Getting adjusted was not as difficult for me as it had been

in Venezuela. Everyone was helpful and friendly. I was able to drive the sisters' truck. In the beginning, I was to observe, perfect my Spanish, and accompany the team as they went about their work. I attended a youth retreat. It was modeled after the Cursillo and Search movements, with youth presenters, singing and games. The purpose was to inspire the youth to form a personal relationship with Christ and then go out and serve others. I was impressed with an event held on Saturday night. All the retreat participants were led into a room that was partially darkened. In candlelight only, the retreat team had created a tableau of the Last Supper. They were dressed in first-century garb with a table in front of them, posed as Jesus and the Apostles. As we gazed at the scene, music filled the air and everyone started to sing. Eventually, the people in the scene started to move and circulate in the room. There was so much joy in one place. It was sincerely a beautiful expression of the faith of these young people. I was touched.

We traveled out of Buenavista for special events. We sometimes drove for hours through fields on an indiscernible road to reach a small group of people to say Mass. We went up the mountain to reach a place of pilgrimage called Apo. High in the mountains was an old church. We went there to honor Mary, the Mother of God, the town's patroness. The people sang, showing their great devotion to Mary. I was cautioned to never turn my back towards Mary, even as we left the church, walking backward, never wanting to show our backsides to the Holy Mother.

The Masses outdoors with the people who had nothing made the gospel stories come alive to me: the story of the lost coin, the Good Shepherd, and the treasure in the field. Because the gospel was written within a rural culture, these stories fit here better than in a suburban church on a crowded highway.

In Buenavista, the hilly streets made it difficult for me to walk very far. When it rained, the streets were pure mud, and everyone had to walk carefully. I slept in a wooden frame bed with a good mattress and a mosquito net. I was getting to know my way around and making friends. But my leg was aching, and my right knee was somewhat wobbly. One evening I heated water on the stove to make a hot pack for my aching leg. But the bowl of water splashed on the floor, and I slipped and fell.

It was a bad fall on a cement floor. I lay there while the sisters went to get the local doctor. He came after dark and straightened out my leg stating nothing was broken. But I couldn't put weight on it and the pain was tremendous. The sisters helped me to the couch where I slept all night. They decided to take me for an X-ray in the morning. The only way to get me to Apatzingán, the largest city near us which was fifteen miles away, was in the back of a pickup truck. They gently carried me on the coffee table to keep my leg straight. I was in tears the whole way. The sun was bright, and I lay on the back of the truck with the sun in my face. One of the neighbors came along and held an umbrella over my face.

Upon reaching the hospital, things were very crazy. They put me on a cot and brought out an X-ray machine that looked like it was left over from World War II. When the X-ray was read, the sad news was that my right hip was fractured. Fr. Eugene visited and told me they would try to get me home to Ohio. But I didn't want to leave. I had only been there for six weeks! I wanted to help but also knew I would need time to recover. Father Eugene called the States and tried to find a way to get me on a plane. The only solution offered was to buy nine seats on a flight so that the stretcher could go in the plane. That was impossible, so I stayed a week in the hospital. An orthopedic Doctor came who knew something about *Osteogenesis Imperfecta*. He surmised that I couldn't travel and shouldn't undergo major surgery there in Mexico without family support. He decided placing the leg in traction was the best course of treatment. This would allow the bone to heal over time and keep it immobile.

That treatment involved a fifteen-minute procedure in which they drilled a pin through my lower femur. With it in place, the traction weight would pull my knee up at an angle so my hip bone would be properly aligned. Fr. Eugene, the leader of our missionary team, was enlisted to engineer a metal bed frame so that I could be moved back to the village to stay with a family. The weight would hang on the bed frame pulling my leg. In this case, the weight was a kilo of nails. By the end of the week, I moved back to Buenavista. A lady in the parish opened her home to me. The priests had a cook and she brought me food every day, so the family didn't have to cook for me. Fortunately, I was not in a lot of pain.

It wasn't all tragic. I was the belle of the state hospital. All the young interns came to visit. They had never had a patient with blue eyes before, and they flirted with me shamelessly. Some even came to the house after I left the hospital. There was always a lot of joking around. I was accustomed to being laid low. I did my best to get through this unbelievable ordeal. To break a hip anytime is a tragedy, but to do it in Mexico was a cruel fate.

When I reached the village and got settled in my new living arrangement, I studied more Spanish, read, and painted miniature watercolor paintings. I kept myself entertained for the most part. I couldn't understand the television programs because they talked too fast. However, I had many visitors, and the orthopedic doctor came once a week to the house to monitor my progress.

I never left the bed for six weeks. Sometimes I cried and tears got in my ears. I had come to Mexico to serve the poor, but they ended up serving me. As we were nearing Christmas, Father Jesse held a retreat for the mission team. By then, I was on crutches. I knew I'd need physical therapy, so plans were made for me to return home.

I wrote this poem during that day of quiet and prayer:

I came to Mexico
to learn the culture
to share the gospel
to live in community
to do without extravagance
to share my being
to visit the sick
I have been here 50 days
and have just begun

I have cried from sadness, disappointment
and with joy.
the tears of an American.
I've shared these tears with Otilia,
Abigail, and the Sisters,
women alike
No cultural differences

In the ranchos
there is neither water, nor light,
only the stars
and the words of love, comfort, encouragement
from the voices of Jesse, Margarita.
They live and preach the gospel, and I too, learn
to breathe its fresh new fragrance.
"Come to me all you who are weary."
And I have been weary with them.
I've shared the gospel.

The community spread itself
north and south, (abajo y arriba).
The people live in communion
the saints and the sinners.
I have been in the hospital six days
My hip is broken
I can neither sit nor stand
and these ten miles from Buenavista
no distance make
for the women of Jerusalem
accompanied Jesus
as he carried his cross

and the people of Buenavista
are with me here.

In the United States even the poor
buy paper diapers.
My knowledge of the world
would not let me accept that,
so I came to Mexico
to live a simpler life.
I have three changes of clothes
I use the same bar of soap to wash
my body
my clothes
my hair
I am totally dependent on those
who assist me
I have been in bed for six days
and have at least fifty more to go
living simply
while others struggle
just miles from here
to simply live.

"My being rejoices in God my Savior"
The words of Mary
My challenge
I was made imperfect so that
the love of God
would heal me and release me from
the bonds of crooked bones,
constant pain,
dreaded loneliness
But rather than perish
I became a missionary
I carry the sacred message of Jesus
to those around me
I am content amid sickness
and my being is whole again.

146

Living Without Bubble Wrap

27

Goodbye to Mexico,
Hello Charlotte

My storehouse being burnt down
Nothing obstructs my view of the moon
— Thich Nhat Hanh

As soon as the doctor took me out of traction, I was able to sit up in a wheelchair. Progress, yes, but too much pain to bear. Muscles that hadn't been used for six weeks began to cry out. I was happy to be out of bed, but the pain was taking away my joy. It was time for the Feast of Our Lady of Guadalupe. This feast is more important than Christmas for the Mexican people. One of my new friends, Lupita, pushed my wheelchair through the unpaved streets so that I could attend some of the events.

It was indeed a poor person's spectacle. People dressed up as the Holy Family or a scene from the life of Jesus and stood, in costume on the back of pick-up trucks. The town's residents gathered to view these tableaus in the street. Children with their parents enjoyed all the revelry. Some rode horses through the town square. It concluded with a special Mass at the church. For this, folk dressed as Mary and Joseph as if they were on the way to Bethlehem. The men wore cowboy hats, and even the children painted mustaches on their faces to look like St. Joseph. I was honored to be part of this cultural phenomenon.

In mid-December, Father Jesse drove me to catch the plane to Mexico City. I was still using crutches or a wheelchair. Maria took care of me in Mexico City until I could get on the plane to Cleveland. I still couldn't walk, so they had to carry me up the steps of the plane and I sat still the entire trip. I wasn't in pain, just a little self-conscious. When I finally got to Cleveland, it was below freezing. I had gone from eighty degrees in Mexico to thirty degrees in one day. It was a lot for my body to adjust. I came home with small gifts I picked up in Mexico City for my family that made it the best Christmas ever. Friends and family were so happy to see me again. Soon I had to deal with snow on the ground with crutches. It was not an easy time, but with rest, prayer, and friends to help, I was fine.

Even though the 'lay' missionary experience in Mexico was over, I wasn't finished with the lay volunteer group. I called Harold Grant and asked him for another assignment, admitting that perhaps I did need to stay in the States. He offered me the chance to work with refugees in Charlotte, North Carolina. I thought if I couldn't live in another country, I could at least pretend I was. I was ready to go by February.

> *The Missionary Cenacle makes you a light in dark places, makes you the strength of the weak; a tree under which the poor and oppressed and the hearts that are tormented may receive refreshment. (Fr. Thomas Judge)*

At the mid-year retreat in February, the volunteer group took the Myers-Briggs personality inventory. Harold Grant was a psychologist. According to the results, my personality fell into the category of 'extroverted feelers.' That means that I show my emotions easily and get most of my energy from being with others. How true! I began to understand more about why certain people were uncomfortable with me; not everyone was extroverted and not everyone craved the attention of the group. I was growing in self-knowledge. I still had a powerful desire to serve and get along better with others. I started my new position in the refugee office in Charlotte with new insights and the humility that comes with learning to live with my physical limitations.

A woman in a long sarong stood at the top of the escalator looking confused. Hello, America. I scampered to the Up escalator to help her. She needed to step down onto the moving stairway with her two young teens following behind.

"Hello! Welcome. I'm Mary from Catholic Charities. I'll take you to your new home."

A nod and a smile. We proceeded to the baggage office to retrieve her blue box covered with blue plastic and tied with string. This is all they brought with them from the camp in Thailand. One box containing some clothing, cooking utensils, spices, and trinkets of remembrance, their lives forever altered by war. Her most valuable item was around her neck in pure gold. If you wear your treasure, it is less likely to be lost.

This was the beginning of this Khmer family's life in Charlotte, NC, U.S.A. Their country of Cambodia was so far away. They were refugees from Southeast Asia. Most of them walked from Cambodia to Thailand for safety, where they lived in U.N. refugee camps for several years before the U.S. accepted them for resettlement. I was lucky enough to meet these new Americans: Khann Hoy and her children, So, and Pheap. Heng Seng, Pheng Loeur, Thoeun Chhuon, and more shared their new lives with us. The names sounded so odd at first, but in time I learned them all and a few words in their Khmer language. It was 1984. In April 1975, a dictator by the name of Pol Pot and his crew had taken over the country, sending educated citizens to the countryside to plant rice and work the fields. Civilization, as they knew it, came to a halt. Universities closed; government offices were now bamboo huts in the jungle.

"Cheers," "Family Ties," and "The Cosby Show" demonstrated American life on TV. It was up to me as a social worker to introduce these traumatized third-world refugees to their new lives in the United States. At the Catholic Charities Refugee resettlement office, we worked as a team. Some set up houses with donated furniture, dishes, and curtains. The families had to be introduced to cars and flush toilets. If it was Christmas time, their home was equipped with a Christmas tree. As Buddhists, they had no idea what it meant. They usually put the tree out on the porch and left it up all summer. Other staff members found them jobs – washing trucks, dry cleaning, and assembly work in small factories. Others taught English and citizenship classes so that when the time came, they would pass the citizenship exam. We drove them around town to the Health Department and Food Stamp offices. Connections were made and the fast pace of American life had to be overwhelming for them.

Khann Hoy thought it was funny how many times she was asked to state her birthdate. In their culture, they did not keep track of such nonsense. Children had to be vaccinated and enrolled in schools where the aides spoke their language in ESL classes. Khann was often perplexed, but under stress, Asians smiled. Their smiles covered the pain of relocation and loss. They lost their family members, their homes, and their country. We tried to protect them and care for them and soon learned we needed to provide for their own cultural expressions.

The film "The Killing Fields" aptly tells their story better than I can. I took Khann Hoy and her children to see the movie. With tears in their eyes, they pointed at the screen saying, "The same me." I came to love my home visits to them, the smell of food cooking, shoes left at the front door, and the endless smiles.

Besides Cambodians, we also resettled Vietnamese, Hmong, and Ethiopian families. I could live in Charlotte but pretend I was in another country. Some of the Vietnamese were Catholic, and I was asked to be a Godmother for a new American/ Vietnamese baby. Most were Buddhist. The largest number was from Cambodia at that time. For their mental health, we set up a Buddhist Temple with two Cambodian monks and two nuns who were also refugees. We joined them for religious holidays, listened to them chant, and smelled the incense. Prayer was important to these gentle people. To honor her, they named the Temple for the Catholic sister who headed up the Catholic Charities Resettlement Office.

My body felt so large and clumsy next to theirs. They sat with knees bent on their heels often, a position I could not master. They were quiet while I was loud. They held their bodies with such poise. They moved gracefully, making every move intentional. I envied their composure. Many of their cultural traditions were hard to replicate in America. And they had so much to learn about ours.

I was elated to attend the wedding of Chen Tin and Sophan Hak. The bride was dressed in a costume that looked like a Bollywood dancer with her midriff showing, lots of bangles, and a flowing skirt. She wore jewels in her hair and kept her hands folded in front of her chest. Her bridegroom wore a more traditional Western dress. I learned that the Chinese influence was strong in their culture. The food at the reception was traditional Chinese. Everyone at the wedding was serenely joyful. The children were well-behaved.

I learned early that their branch of Buddhism believes that the spiritual essence of the person flows out the top of their head. I was not to touch the tops of a child's head or it would be rude. To pick up a person's spirit, they would give the person a little sniff. They learned this was not western custom, so they didn't do it to us. From my journal:

> *"The Cambodian New Year celebration at the Temple. We are all dressed up and under the blooming dogwoods – a celebration of being Cambodian, being alive. They danced. They played games, they politely offered food. They invented the word 'hospitality.' How good it is – knowing their history brought tears to my eyes. Sherry and I took them a basket of fruit, and the Buddhist nuns sat down and blessed it. The monk sat serenely in his chair until I came near him. He jumped up – he may not know that I know he can't let a woman touch him. My Cambodian friend hugged me when he saw me – we had been lost on the highway together on Friday. Such beautiful people! They have so much to teach me."*

I primarily taught English but was assigned other duties. One assignment was to work with an elderly Vietnamese man who was thin and frail-looking. I was told he was depressed. I typically went to his house to spend time with him. I wasn't sure what to do, not being a trained therapist, but I smiled at him, and he smiled back at me. I could only imagine what he had been through. Maybe he had been a soldier, or a teacher, or a shoe salesman. It didn't matter. We shared that present moment. He was so very sad. My visits were regular, and I showed him that I cared by checking on him.

One of my favorite Ethiopian families consisted of a father, a mother, and four children. The youngest child was born with Down's syndrome. His name was Zachary. His three older sisters doted on him and looked out for him. The father worked but would take time off if one of the children had a medical appointment. He could speak some English. One day I took Dad and Zachary to the clinic. It was a follow-up visit after a diagnosed ear infection. Time dragged on as if we were children waiting for Christmas. When we finally got into the exam room, the doctor investigated the child's ears. Then he looked at the father, realizing his English was not so good, he slowly asked, "Have you been putting the liquid medicine in the child's ears?"

"Yes. I put in the medicine," the father replied.

"I'm so sorry, but you were to put the medicine in his mouth, not his ears."

Another cultural clash, and of course, it made sense. Dad knew the problem was in the ears, so why wouldn't the medicine go in there? We got a new prescription and I carefully explained to the family how to give the medicine. An honest mistake. I just wanted to wrap my arms around this family as they made baby steps into American life.

This volunteer commitment lasted eighteen months. I shared a house with two other volunteers, and we had a lot of fun. We redecorated the house, painting the walls tomato red. We dated some guys and went to disco bars. Sharon went on to obtain her Master of Social Work degree. Kate moved to Chicago where she pursued work with the homeless. For myself, I yearned for a position more in tune with my Catholic faith.

The refugee work was winding down, and I learned there

was a volunteer position with the Trinitarians in Pensacola, Florida. Sister Gail wanted to bring three missionary volunteers to Pensacola to run an outreach center for the poor. After I visited Pensacola for an interview and saw the beaches, I was sold. It was hard to say goodbye to close friends in Charlotte, especially some of the Cambodian families that had welcomed me into their homes. I cried all the way out of Charlotte on the highway. I didn't know then, but I would spend the next twenty-five years in Pensacola, Florida.

28

Florida Sun

Pensacola gleams in the sunshine, especially when driving along the bay, over the bridge through Gulf Breeze to the beach. I had no car of my own at first, so my mom picked me up in Charlotte and drove me to Pensacola so she could see my new place. I was to live with two other Missionary Cenacle Volunteers, Maribeth, and Gerry, in a convent with Sister Maureen, a sister of Charity. The convent was a relic of the past, as was Sister Maureen. Our job was to set up an Outreach Center for the poor in an old school building on the east side of Pensacola. It was in a poor African-American neighborhood. Maribeth was put in charge of food distribution, Gerrie was to take responsibility for financial aid for people who needed it, and I was to run the clothing room. Sister Maureen had other duties at St. Joseph Church and worked part-time with us at the Outreach Center because she knew the resources and people in the neighborhood. Our ages spanned four decades with Maribeth only in her twenties, just out of college; Gerry was in her forties, and I was thirty. Sister Maureen was in her fifties, but full of life and she could be fun. We worked hard during the week and spent weekends at the beach.

Again, I was to learn about another type of poverty. Pensacola is beautiful with great weather and an interesting history, but the poor live in substandard houses, close to the city center. The houses are wood on blocks leaving a shaky foundation and space for vermin to congregate. Many of the older African-American women used to be maids but their employers moved away. This left them without skills and too young for social security, and only if the families they worked for had paid into it. There were few employment opportunities for unskilled workers. Some of them worked as hotel staff at the beach hotels, but that was a ten-mile drive from home. In the neighborhood by the Outreach

Center, most received welfare and food stamps. One day a week we received day-old bread. A group of senior citizens came on Wednesdays to our Outreach Center to get bread from us and play bingo. We called them the "Bread People" and they took up a special place in our hearts. We interviewed other clients to figure out the extent of their needs. On busy days we served fifty families, spreading our limited funds thin.

We worked regular hours, so our evenings were free. Marybeth and I joined a Catholic singles group. They had many social activities, with limited spiritual focus. I joined the Social Justice Commission of the Diocese of Pensacola-Tallahassee. We tried to put some attention on peacemaking in the world and income inequality, but people who live near the beach are not looking for social justice; they just want to relax. I met some lifelong friends working on that committee. We learned that contras from Honduras and El Salvador were being trained at the nearby Hurlburt Field Air Force Base. U.S. policy in Latin America tended towards support of the status quo and kept money in the hands of the few. We were upset at the use of our military to oppress the people of Central America. We met every Sunday afternoon to hold signs outside the military base to show our concerns.

"Get a job! Go back to your own town!" were just some of the words yelled at us as we stood witness. In my mind I said, *I have a job. This is where I live.* Our banner said, "Violence ends where love begins," the slogan of Pax Christi USA, a Catholic peace group.

At the end of our volunteer year, Maribeth decided to join the convent and headed off to Arkansas. Gerrie decided to stay for another year, and I wanted to get my own apartment and look for a paying job after three years of volunteer work. I made some contacts with other social workers through Catholic Charities and started graduate school to become a counselor. The world was opening for me in new ways. Before landing a full-time position, I worked in the pre-school for refugee children started by the Diocese of Pensacola-Tallahassee. The children we served were from Cambodia and Viet Nam. There were a few

Spanish-speaking kids, so they hired me for my Spanish fluency. Meanwhile, I looked for another social work job. I thought if I had to work a difficult job, at least I could de-stress at the beach.

In November of 1986, I was hired to do Special Needs adoption for the State of Florida, the Department of Health, and Human Services. I knew something about adoption since my sister, Maggie had adopted two infants in the seventies. My supervisor, another Carol, asked me during the interview.

"How religious are you? I see you have had many jobs associated with the church. Are you going to proselytize our clients?"

"Oh, no. My faith inspires me to serve others. It's like the wind behind my sails."

She told me later that statement assured her I was not a fanatic. And I got the job.

The work included not only finding families for emotionally disturbed children but also doing home studies for divorce custody when there was a dispute between parents. Some of the adoptions occurred in an unconventional way. One police officer was given a baby in a deli. Another time, a young mother gave her child to a truck driver she met along the highway. The truck driver had the child for eight years before making it legal. My task was to check out the situation and recommend to the judge if it should become legal. This took me to all the different neighborhoods in Pensacola.

One of the older children in foster care became my special cause. He was a thirteen-year-old boy named Lennie. When I met him, he was living in a group home run by the local mental health center. His father was in a mental facility. He raised him on his own for twelve years and worked as a janitor at a Baptist church. Born in Missouri, Lennie's mother had left his dad when Lennie was just an infant. They made their way to Florida, sometimes living in the car, seeking employment. But this time, his father had a severe case of amnesia. Lennie had been put in a children's home in Tallahassee because of behavior problems at school. In the meantime, his dad ended up in Pensacola in a mental ward. When the caseworker brought the two together, the dad didn't recognize Lennie. They tried everything including sodium pentothal to jog his memory. Nothing worked. So, it was the state's responsibility to sever the father's legal rights and place Lennie for adoption.

I received a stack of psychological reports on Lennie and his father. As I got to know Lennie, I found him to have a joyful, puppy-like personality, eager to please and eager for a family. He had a small build and loved hugs. I met with his teachers at the special school he attended, located on the grounds of Lakeview Center, a comprehensive community mental health agency. As charming as Lennie could be, he was also hard to manage. Sometimes he ran away for two or three days. I was worried. Then he'd come back with lice and hungry. He was not aggressive and was bullied for his small size and the crazy things he would do. In school, he was caught sniffing White-Out, taken from the teacher's desk. He was mischievous as most boys are, but he took it to a dangerous level. In foster care, he moved every few months from group homes to shelters because he didn't follow the rules.

In the summer, I got him a job through a federal youth employment program. He cashed his first paycheck at a local convenience store and bought a case of beer for everyone at the group home, sneaking out at night to do so. Near the group home was a gas station known for selling beer to minors called "Beer City." The staff found the case of beer outside his bedroom window, all emptied by then.

One of the ways we matched families and children was to have a meet-and-greet party. The approved families would come, and I would bring Lennie. Other caseworkers would bring their kids eligible for adoption. In sharing a meal, people could meet different kids to see if they clicked. Lennie's birth mother was Latina. He had nice brown eyes and light brown skin. A family in Fort Walton Beach met him at the party. Mrs. Johnson was Latina and Mr. Johnson was in the military. They had one daughter and felt they wanted to expand their family through adoption. They met Lennie and were smitten. I introduced the Johnsons to Lennie's teachers, showed them his psychological profile, and arranged visits. Lennie really wanted to be loved. He was on his best behavior. After a few weekend visits, it was decided this was a good match.

It was as if the Johnsons didn't hear a word I said. They knew he was at risk for running away, was a slow learner, and there would be an adjustment period. Lennie needed close supervision. Both parents worked. One day they came home from school to find Lennie in bed with their ten-year-old daughter. I don't have all the details, but I presume Lennie didn't know about family boundaries. He had never had a sister. He wanted comfort. I also had no information previously that he was sexually abused or acting out in that way. In retrospect, I should have had the Johnsons say explicitly to Lennie, "No going in your sister's room. Ever!" And I should have told the Johnsons he needed twenty-four-hour supervision.

It was up to me to find Lennie a place to live and the emotional support to get through this loss. He got a bed at the Lakeview shelter, not a treatment facility but a holding place for kids who were in between homes. He spent a lot of time there. I got to know the staff and other residents as well. I drove Lennie to weekly appointments with a psychologist. He was diagnosed with ADHD and low intelligence. This was a kid who could thrive in the right environment. Lennie did have one contact in the Pensacola community besides me. That was Alex and his wife. Alex knew his dad from the Baptist church and had watched him over the years. Lennie could spend weekends with them from time to time, but they were not open to adoption.

When Lennie was fifteen or sixteen, we tried another family. They were an older couple, both recovering alcoholics, both had spent time in prison. They went through our adoption class and were open to a teenage boy. The philosophy of Special Needs adoption is to match up families and children who are somewhat alike. Middle-class families with successful children headed to college don't usually work out with these kids. This couple was a viable choice for Lennie. They knew the life of hard knocks, and he did all right there for many months. They built a new house in Ponce de Leon, Florida, after their house in Pensacola burned down. It was closer to where Mrs. B grew up. She had five beautiful grown daughters near there. Therefore, there would be more family support for Lennie.

But as is often the case, violence lies beneath the surface of good people. Mr. B lost his temper and hit Lennie. We had to take Lennie back into Foster Care. I picked him up on a rainy day in July and we rode the ninety miles back to Pensacola in a terrible thunderstorm. It echoed what we were feeling; angry. afraid of the future. Hopeless. I found a caring foster home for Lennie where he remained until he turned eighteen. This was a family of experienced foster parents who had more tolerance for odd behaviors. Yet it was a safe family with rules and a close relationship with our agency. The father, Fred, was in a wheelchair because of a spinal injury, so he was home all day long. They loved Lennie and sheltered him several times before he moved in. He aged out of the foster care system, having never been successfully adopted.

I ran into him in town one day in 1992. He told me he was sharing a trailer with a guy he met on the west side of Pensacola. He was receiving a disability check but hadn't given up on getting a job. He didn't have a car, so I drove him around sometimes. He appreciated all my help over the years and even asked me to help him fill out job applications and be a reference. He was in touch with the family in Ponce de Leon. There were no bad feelings about the adoption failure; he thought of them as family.

About five years later he showed up in an 18-wheeler truck. I was working at the school at Lakeview where he had attended when he was in middle school. He came back to look for old friends. He looked clean and more muscular. He told me he was married and divorced with two kids. Now he drove long haul loads from coast to coast. I couldn't believe it! He parked the truck outside the school and let our current students crawl up into the cab. He was quite proud of himself, and I was proud of him as well. He had the habit of staying awake all night so I could imagine him trucking through the night. Although he was never legally adopted, he made friends all over the Florida panhandle. And he thought of me as family.

But what does that mean? From my heart, it means hope when there is only despair. Showing up when there is a court appearance, a birthday, a wake. Lennie is the kind of person my mother taught me to love, not just to do my job, but because I was also fulfilling my mission to reach out to the abandoned.

29

What Family Means

Let mutual love continue. Do not neglect hospitality, for through it some have unknowingly entertained angels.
(Hebrews 13:1-2)

Meanwhile, in Elyria, Ohio, my mom's household had become a family of Lennies. It started when I went away to college in 1971. My mom, a widow, still lived in my childhood home with four bedrooms. She was used to having a brood of children, but then in her 50s with all of us gone, she heard of others in need. She took in one of the earliest 'clients' of Betterway, Inc. when she was released from her commitment to the group home. Her name is Angie, and she couldn't return home to Cleveland. Mom became a licensed foster home to let Angie move in. When I came home for Christmas break, Angie was there with us at the Christmas parties as one of the family. She stayed with Mom for a couple of years, finishing high school. Our family grew. Family means being there for someone.

My Mom rarely slowed down. She enjoyed having people in her home. She would benefit from non-profit agencies who gave away clothing. The front door was never locked. In time, everyone in town knew "Gert" could find someone a bed or a new pair of shoes.

As I continued my college years, more girls came. Mom offered to take in pregnant girls as they were kicked out of their homes. Mom knew everyone in our town and the word got out that Gert had room. She welcomed Kathy, a pregnant redhead, and Kim. When the babies were born, social workers helped the girls get their own apartments, but they were always welcome to come back to Twelfth Street for support and a meal. Family is offering a home-cooked meal.

Mom became the overflow house for the battered women's shelter. Some stayed for weeks, others only a day, but each one was brought into the family circle. When workers from Betterway needed a place to get away, they came over for respite from troubled teens. Mom never locked her door.

Many staff members became her friends. Mary Rossi, a vibrant Italian American from Little Italy on the east side of Cleveland was one. Mary loved food and could describe green beans as if they were caviar. Then followed Regina, hired by St. Mary's Church to be a religious education teacher. With Regina, Mom shared her love of the church and all kinds of social ministry. The house was often full of lively conversation on theology and social causes. Family means sharing interests.

Through church friends, Mom heard about Rose. She had been released from a mental hospital in Columbus upon turning 18. She couldn't live at home because she didn't get along with her mother. Upon entering the house, she asked my mom, "Are you a psychiatric social worker?"

Mom answered, "No, I'm just a mom." Rose was supposed to stay for two weeks but she stayed for nine years. During that time, Rose became a fixture. She had many friends from the outpatient mental health center, and all of them visited. Rose dated lots of guys and we got to know them too. One of them was Larry, diagnosed with paranoid schizophrenia. He told me once that he had checked the records at the health department and he had a right to live at our house because he was married to my mother! Rose completed her Associate Degree at our community college and got her first job. I liked Rose's adventurous spirit. After a severe snowstorm, she was the first one out on the treacherous roads, dying to get out of the house. When Rose finally moved out, she was angry. I learned that for some people it's hard to say goodbye when things are going well. Instead, people leave mad because it is easier. Family means putting up with each other.

I had been reading the writing of Dorothy Day, her autobiographies, *The Long Loneliness*, and *From Union Square to Rome*.

My desire to work with the poor was shared with my mom. Mom had copies of the Catholic Worker newspaper at her store. We were learning about non-violence, contemplative spirituality, and homelessness. Mom didn't feel right if someone needed a place to stay if she had empty bedrooms. She made simple meals for everyone and did their wash.

Her tent grew increasingly larger. One summer, four young Bible salesmen went to St. Mary's asking for recommendations on where to stay in Elyria. They were all from California, employed to sell books door-to-door for a Nashville publishing house. I was home for the summer to enjoy all the fun. She took in all four. They were dropped off by a sales Manager and had never really been away from home. Mark was a member of the Seventh-Day Adventist Church. He never worked on Saturday, their Sabbath, but spent the day quietly, not even listening to secular music on that day. We learned about their faith and practices. Miguel was a bit more savvy, so moved on after a month. He wasn't willing to go door-to-door for such low pay. Dennis was a military brat who grew up all over the world, but his social skills were lacking. For fun, he would sit in the bean bag chair in the middle of the living room and read the dictionary aloud. Kevin was the only one with a salesman personality. He was the social butterfly of the group. Mom fed them and did their laundry, too. She enjoyed their company in the evenings. She also cheered them on in their sales pursuit. At the end of summer, they flew home with the hard-earned cash.

A German carpenter showed up one year and fixed everything that needed fixing at the house. He had a strong accent and, just as he appeared out of nowhere, he disappeared one day, never to be heard from again. We all enjoyed Hartmut, but sometimes we had to remind him to bathe. Part of me believes he was a spy of some sort, in a period of laying low.

The social worker at Elyria Memorial Hospital heard of Mom and asked her to take in a woman who had been sleeping on the floor of the waiting room. Her husband, a long-haul truck driver, had a massive heart attack on the Interstate near Elyria.

They were from another state and the wife had no money for a hotel. Mom gave her a room of her own for a few days and listened to her woes. No exchange of money was necessary.

My nephews, Michael and John, stayed with Mom in between apartments. Once Michael brought over a guy he met at a café that was down on his luck. He turned out to be a one-nighter who wet the bed. Thanks, Michael.

Mom had income from working at the bookstore and social security. Her biggest expenses were the gas bill and her car. She lived month to month and never expected payment. Rose's dad gave her twenty dollars a week for years.

Mom took everyone under her large wings. They made her laugh. And they made her cry. She wrote a letter to God every night in her journal, thanking him for his blessings and asking him to fix a few things. Nearly 100 different people showed up for her love. Sometimes we called her "Mother Superior."

> *"Come you who are blessed by my Father. Inherit the kingdom prepared for you from the foundation of the world. For I was hungry, and you gave me food, I was thirsty and you have me drink, a stranger and you welcomed me, naked and you clothed me, in prison and you visited me. Whatever you did for one of these least brothers of mine, you did for me."*
> Matthew 25:34-36, 40.

30

The Tears of a Clown

It was a good day when I ate and washed a few dishes. That's how bad my depression got. Misery and wretchedness overcame me. At the same time, I was still going to work and passing as fine. I was over thirty. Most of my old friends from Ohio and Pensacola were married with children. I had decided to get out of my adoption job for one that was less emotional. There was an opening in foster home recruiting. I had a private office but some days I would sit there and doodle. I made a few phone calls to prospective foster parents and set up meetings. No one was looking over my shoulder. There were no quotas to meet. I was also taking graduate classes at Troy State University. I muddled through my days. I moved papers around on my desk and ate lunch at Morrison's Cafeteria, usually alone. I was still getting over my break-up with Jay. Even though ending our relationship was my idea, I still felt sad. I knew it would be hard to meet someone new. My thoughts were swimming around my head with no shore on which to land. I talked to my sister, Anne, in Pittsburgh. She encouraged me to walk to relieve stress.

Without Jay in my life, I planned to fly home to Elyria for Christmas. In October, I approached my new supervisor. "Barbara, I need to get a plane ticket for Christmas, what days may I have off?"

"Oh, Mary, I give priority to those who have children. We'll have to see," she responded.

I went back to my office, closed the door, and started to cry. This was the first time I ever cried at work. I had, up until then, kept the charade going. *"People say I'm the life of the party because I tell a joke or two, I may be laughing loud and hardy, but deep inside I'm blue."* sang Smokey Robinson. I smiled all the time. I pushed myself to participate. I was a good actress.

But I was not okay. I didn't have children, nor was there a possibility of having children. I was alone. Inside my heart was in pieces. I wanted to say to Barbara, *"But I'm a child. I deserve to be with my family!"* I have spent five years giving others the opportunity to have children through adoption. I photographed happy families coming together for that final court date when their adoptions were finalized. *It's not fair. I'd be a good mother, I thought. I'm supposed to have a family of my own. But right now, I'm single and thirty-something. This is hard. I need help!*

I decided to call a therapist and get help. I remembered Erika, a woman in class at Troy State. She told me she worked with women who were having fertility problems. She and I also talked about my work in adoptions. I called her number. I didn't care about the cost. I had health insurance, and I was pretty sure there would be a hefty co-pay. I set an appointment to see Erika after work the following Tuesday. When I got home that evening, I wrote out some of my thoughts in my journal. I took a walk. I listened to music. Mary Chapin Carpenter, I think.

I traveled to Erika's house where she had a private room in the back for appointments. I knocked on the door. She popped out and asked me to wait. I stood in her backyard and looked at the live oak trees. Soon another woman came outside and left, and I was invited in. I sat down and stared at the starlight mints in the candy dish. She inquired about what I wanted to talk about.

I said, "I'm here because I ended my two-year relationship with my boyfriend, I can't have children because of an unwanted hysterectomy, and I have a stressful job." I thought my hormones were messed up because of the hysterectomy, "Can you help?"

As tears began to flow, she gently listened and suggested that I look at my life like it's a movie and that we needed to just freeze this frame. She contracted with me for weekly sessions for several weeks and then we'd see how much more time was needed. I talked, I cried, I talked some more. We met together for three years. I did have a few visits with a psychiatrist for medication.

Eventually, I brought in my childhood photo album and talked about the dreams I had of becoming a mother. Those currents in my subconscious were strong. We sang ditties like *"First comes love, then comes marriage, then comes babies in a baby carriage."* As young Catholics, we were told that if you visited a church for the first time, you could make a wish. Traveling through Europe in 1977, I wished at every church to have a child. I wanted children so badly. Being the youngest in the family, I became an aunt at age eight. I played with baby dolls. I was babysitting at age eleven. It was just natural that I wanted children. Erika helped me to grieve that loss. I began to feel hollow inside.

We talked about my father's death and my mother's commitment to the homeless. When my birthday came one year, I told her I wanted to give my friends a present for being so good to me. My idea was to celebrate friendship. Erika shook her head. "Not a good idea Mary." She led me to understand my codependency. I was more comfortable giving than receiving. She encouraged me to love and take care of myself. No one before her had ever emphasized self-care to me. In my family, it was work, work, work and give, give, give. There are people who need you. I was always on a mission. I had to struggle to make time for myself. It was a foreign concept.

Erika was there for me as I completed my graduate degree in Counseling and started a counseling internship. She held my hand as I bought my first house. I had a lot of things to work through. Erike often spent more than an hour with me. While waiting in her backyard, I looked up at the tree branches and saw my crooked arms and legs. I told her about it and she asked me to bring in some of the watercolor paintings I'd been painting. In the roots of trees, I used alizarin crimson for color. Many of the trees I painted had long wavy limbs. Erika looked at my paintings and pointed to the red in the tree roots. She indicated that it represented the anger I felt about my bones. She directed me to use my art to express my feelings more directly instead of hiding my anger in the landscapes so I made an anger collage. I also did an angry self-portrait. These activities were extremely helpful to me to dislodge internal feelings.

One counseling teacher told me that you had to sit on both sides of the desk to be a good counselor. I was a patient and a therapist. I learned my lessons well. Grief is also developmental. As an eleven-year-old when my father died, I grieved the loss as an eleven-year-old. Much later, I had to come to terms with that loss as an adult woman. Erika guided me as I did the work. All the other losses, my desire for a boyfriend (always a bridesmaid, never a bride), the pain of an unexpected hysterectomy, the pain of broken bones, the loss of dreams. I was able to take my time, to do my artwork, journal, cry, talk to friends, and process it all during my time with Erika.

The journey was long and arduous, but the clarity I gained was important. I became a wiser person.

31

Play Therapy

$\mathcal{P}$lay is the work of children.
Jean Piaget

My mentor and friend, Lorainne introduced me to Play Therapy. Play is the language of children. Playing is a very natural way for children to deal with the challenges they feel every day, as well as emotional problems. If I were to continue to work with children in therapy, I'd need to know Play Therapy. During my Internship with Lorainne, she insisted that I attend a "Creative Arts and Play Therapy" workshop by Michael DeMaria, Ph D.

The two-day workshop started with Dr. DeMaria tossing out beach balls into the crowd of fifty attendees. Everyone became involved in keeping the balls in the air. He did this to demonstrate how play affects us all. Our hearts started beating faster and people started to smile. The energy in the room was contagious. I learned a great deal that day that I intended to use with my counseling clients.

Sand play can help a client tap into their subconscious, which may be why going to the beach is relaxing. Playing along with art can further a child's ability to share and heal. One of the activities I used with older children being adopted was to make a life book. Through drawing and coloring, this activity helped the child to answer three questions: "Who am I? What happened to me?" and "Where am I going?" One boy drew a skeleton in a coffin when asked to draw how he felt entering foster care. It was powerful! I was sure I could continue my work with these new therapeutic tools.

The workshop was at the Holiday Inn in Pensacola where they offered a buffet lunch. While in line for food, I struck up a conversation with a man about the pieces of art on the walls. He was animated and engaged easily. We both shared an interest in folk art. We knew some of the same people at Lakeview, the mental health center. I told him I had worked in adoptions and had been at the youth shelter and school there with clients. He was now a school counselor in a public school but had worked at Lakeview as a teacher. In fact, he had taught Lenny. Although we knew the rules of confidentiality, there was no one quite like Lenny, and we shared our stories. The conversation lit a spark — the man I met was Ben.

Ben invited me to an art show, but I couldn't make it. However, when the list of workshop participants came out, he called me for a date, which was the beginning of our romance. I invited him to see the home I had just purchased. The next time we had a date, Ben brought a picnic of shrimp and fixings to a park.

I didn't know his age, but I guess he was a little older than me. He was short in stature with dark expressive eyes and the countenance that lets you know he was really listening. His dark hair and a mustache indicated the Latino heritage. One time I asked him, "How did you miss Vietnam?"

"I didn't. I was in the Air Force and served as a corpsman there for a short time." He answered.

"Oh my God!" I gasped. "I was probably protesting when you were there."

I found out he was a single dad, 45 years of age. His son Benito was 17. That summer I learned more and more about them by spending time with them. Ben liked making things. Benito was on the high school swim team. Ben's parents lived in Pensacola, and they were a close family. Benito was a senior in high school. Ben was off work for the summer. Benito had a serious girlfriend. We enjoyed going to the beach and concerts. That summer, karaoke was popular, and there was an amphitheater at Pensacola Beach where people gathered to sing. I sang the song "Someday Soon" by Judy Collins. Ben met my friends that night and another time he organized a cookout at my new house to get to know my friends.

We decided in October to become engaged and planned a June 1993 wedding.

Part Three: A Soft Landing

32

Two Become Three

Warming up to Benito was a little challenging. He was a teenaged boy, concerned about his looks and his future. He wasn't that interested in me. Benito had been adopted by Ben and his first wife, Linda, but she was not involved in his life for very long. In fact, when they were divorced, Benito was only four years old, and as circumstances would have it, at the time of the divorce, Linda got custody of Benito in Texas. Shortly afterward, there was a tornado in Wichita Falls, Texas and Linda called Ben to come and pick up Benito. Ben was headed to Florida but turned the car around. For the next 10 years, it was just Ben and Benito together. No contact with Linda. Benito didn't need a mother or a stepmother. Ben's mother, Robbie, was the female voice in Benito's head; she was his de facto mother. Ben knew that Benito was going to be pulling away in a few years, so he didn't insist on his involvement in our relationship.

We planned the wedding for June after which Ben and Benito would move into my house in Gulf Breeze. Benito could continue to attend Washington high school in Pensacola even though we were living in Gulf Breeze in another county.

Father Flaherty said, "You are the worst bride I've ever worked with!" Before marriage in the Catholic Church, we were required to go through counseling with the priest and attend a marriage preparation program. Because Ben had been married previously, he also had to submit paperwork showing his marriage and divorce. After taking a personality inventory, we met with the priest to go over issues that might affect our marriage.

During the discussion, Father Flaherty started to agree with Ben on issues such as friendships, communication, and finances. I took issue with that. The session was not going well. Then we discussed how the ceremony would go. Father Flaherty thought we should have a Catholic mass for the wedding, and I did not. As Ben's family is not Catholic, nor are many of our friends, we had decided to have parts of the Catholic mass in the ceremony but not the whole Mass. I did not want guests at our wedding to be denied the Holy Communion. That's when Father Flaherty said, "You are the worst bride I ever worked with. I'm not going to be a part of this ceremony and you can get anyone you want to marry you!" So, we invited Rev. Henry Roberts, a Methodist minister, and Father Pathe to do an Interfaith ceremony in the Catholic Church, St. Joseph's.

Ben emerged as a peacemaker and confidant. He knew when I was emotional, how to step back and let me cry. We invited my entire family to the wedding, which meant travel and hotel arrangements. Pensacola is an inviting destination, nevertheless.

David G. got off the plane carrying a box. He said it was our wedding cake. Behind him came the pilot, co-pilot, and an airline steward, also carrying similar boxes. David made the cake in Cleveland, and it traveled in the overhead compartment all the way to Florida. Everyone on the plane knew they were on a plane with a wedding cake.

We had a lovely wedding with some traditional elements and some not-so-traditional. We entered the church, walking down the aisle together. No one was giving me away! We were there to have our relationship witnessed by others and blessed by God. Before the service *Ave Maria* was sung a beautiful nod to the motherhood of Mary. Benito was his dad's best man; my matron of honor was my best friend, Sherrye. Ben's parents, Gilbert and Robbie, joined my mom in lighting the family candles, a set of three candles. They lit the two on the outside, and after we took our vows, Ben and I lit the middle one showing our unity.

After the ceremony in church, we all went to the reception hall for a buffet lunch. We didn't spend a lot of time taking photographs but took one group photo on the church steps. No alcohol was permitted, so after the reception, we changed our clothes to join family members at Rosie O'Grady's Tavern in downtown Pensacola. Everyone seemed happy for us, and we all had fun laughing and joking.

After a great honeymoon in Cape San Blas on the Florida panhandle, Ben and Benito moved into my house with their life belongings. Still a kid at heart, Benito requested a trip to Six Flags in Atlanta before the summer ended. There we stayed with a cousin of mine who, to be frugal, did not use the A/C that summer. They had asked their kids to decide whether to join the neighborhood pool that summer or have A/C. The kids chose the pool! We sweated the two nights at their house, but it was a nice family getaway to share with Benito before his senior year of high school.

Back home in Gulf Breeze, we began our life together. Benito to high school. Ben and I went to our prospective schools to work with troubled children.

33

The Working Family

hen the morning freshness has been replaced
by the weariness of mid-day,
when the leg muscles quiver under the strain,
the climb seems endless
and suddenly nothing will go quite as you will.
It is then that you must not hesitate.
— Dag Hammarskjold

After all the thank-you notes for wedding gifts were written, it was time for me to learn how to live with two men: Ben and Benito. It's funny to look back on it now, but that first year was tough. I wasn't used to meal planning, but Ben and Benito were, as most men are much more focused on food than I would ever be. Ben was used to getting paid once a month, so it was his habit when he got paid to load up the freezer so they would have food to last until the end of the month. The first meal I cooked for dinner was chicken and pineapple in the wok over rice. The phone rang during dinner. Benito got up to answer it and after the call headed to the bathroom — to throw up! Both Ben and Benito were not used to warm fruit. Another lesson for me. I was an inexperienced cook, and Ben and Benito both had many food preferences.

So many changes! Because I bought my house in 1992, just before meeting Ben, the walls were all off-white, a neutral color to help the owner sell the house. And I'm not much of a decorator. I had some nice things, special paintings, and art pieces, but the house was plain. Ben said I decorated like a nun, My life tends to go on outside the home. Ben was just the opposite, more of a homebody, wanting his surroundings to reflect his life. He spent the first year picking up paint samples at Lowe's and Home

Depot. Each time he went shopping, there were more colors to consider. He set about painting each room a different color.

We had some financial hiccups, too. I was a saver. Ben was just making ends meet, and I soon found out he had more than one outstanding loan. From time to time, his parents loaned him money which he was repaying. I had never owed anyone money. It made me uncomfortable. Consequently, we set up a budget, and with two incomes, we were just fine. Benito was a senior in high school and needed money for swimming, field trips, prom, graduation, this or that as well as college testing. We had to make it a rule that he couldn't ask for money in the morning before we all headed out for work and school. We needed to know the night before. That took some sting out of the requests for money. He was working but had to put gas in the car with that money. Once Ben's mom, Robbie, gave Benito a credit card to buy shoes at a local department store. When the bill came, she learned he had also purchased something for his girlfriend on her card. Teenage boys have an endless appetite for food and for things.

I was still dealing with some depression and seeing Erika. While I cried almost every day, in my heart, I knew our marriage was going to be fine. The depression, despite my happiness in loving Ben, was reoccurring because of all the changes I was going through. I wanted a family, and I got one. Ben's mom was my sounding board. She sat at her kitchen table in Pensacola and managed to listen to all of us. On stressful days at work, if I went to lunch at her house, I could show up and just lie on the couch. No questions asked. She told me if I was frustrated with Ben that he would not change. I knew that. She said he had been the same since eighth grade.

Robbie expressed her happiness with our marriage in two distinct ways. First, she gave Ben a diamond earring from her mother for my engagement ring. And secondly, she told me that my presence in Ben's life was a blessing. He was always looking out for others, but now he had me looking out for him. And she also fed us. On holidays and birthdays, she loved cooking for hordes of people. She made a twenty-two-pound turkey for twelve people. The side dishes were huge; two kinds of pota-toes, cranberry salad, tossed salad, green beans, gravy, shoepeg corn, enough starches to build a house! She kept all the leftovers in the refrigerator in the house and the extra frig in the garage. We were expected to come over the next several days to eat the leftovers. In the Encinias family, providing food is their way of showing love.

Ben is a quiet man, and I am the noisy one. He is a caregiver, too. Since he was in high school, he has taken on responsibilities eagerly. His mother didn't drive, so he became the one to take clothes to the laundromat, do the shopping, and do most of the family errands. His dad often worked out of town; he ran one of the first Job Corps Camps in Maryland while Ben was in his teens.

I gave Ben the opportunity to be a caregiver in our second year of marriage by falling out of bed and breaking a pelvic bone. Ben was leaving for work, and I was going to work later, so I was still in bed. The phone rang, and as I climbed out of the bed to get the phone, my feet got tangled up in the sheets, and I fell. I knew I was hurt. I saw Ben still walking in the yard so banged on the window for him to come and help me. He and our neighbor managed to get me into the car while I screamed in pain. The x-ray at the ER confirmed a fracture. There was noth-ing to be done but go home and wait for it to heal. Even strong pain medication gave me no relief. That was a tough time. Ben had to half-carry me to the bathroom. It was October 1994, and we were supposed to travel to Ohio for my niece's wedding, but we couldn't make it. I was disappointed and hurt but managed.

Benito was doing well at college at Florida State Universi-ty where he secured a job as manager for the FSU swim team. F.S.U. is a big party school, so we knew he was drinking a lot. We spoke with Benito on the phone a great deal; he had broken up with a girlfriend and was sad. All we could do was be there for him when he needed us. Ben had raised him with love and taught him values. He was more ready than most kids to be away from home. He knew how to shop, wash clothes, and clean. Ben taught him everything he needed to know. Benito came home for the summer and worked as a lifeguard.

Benito spent most of Christmas break on the phone with the girl he was dating. I was upset that he had not bought any presents for family members. Ben had to be at the Midnight Christmas service early, and Benito and I were to come later. So, we were home together when I said, "You didn't even think to buy your grandparents a present!" He said some choice words back to me and slammed the door. We traveled to church in separate cars and sat in separate pews. Ben could tell from the altar, where he stood, that something was wrong. When we got home, following a lovely Christmas Eve service at the Methodist Church, Ben sat us down on the couch and told us to work it out. Suffice to say, we did. The rest of Christmas went better. The household was never completely peaceful as Benito and I have strong personalities; we were both going through changes.

That summer, we experienced hurricane Erin together. We stayed home and did not evacuate because we were not ordered to do so. We lived on a peninsula between Pensacola and Pensacola Beach. The rain and wind were fierce. We watched the trees sway and branches flowing in the waves of water down the street. We lost power; and then had to agree on what radio station to tune in to. Of course, Benito wanted music while Ben and I wanted news. Then everything calmed down. The eye of the hurricane passed right over us. We went outside and walked around on our street which was covered with a salad of leaves and branches. The neighborhood was utterly calm. And after about thirty minutes, the wind started up again, even stronger. Back inside, we looked out the window and saw our neighbor's screen surrounding his pool collapse. We were in awe of the power of the storm but thankful we had no damage to our house or cars.

I can't say our first few years of marriage were easy. They were not. But we had love and commitment. We were in for a long journey.

We survived both named and unnamed hurricanes.

<h1 style="text-align:center">34</h1>

It Takes a Village

Marriage did not turn me into a homebody. Ben and I were programmed to do community work by our parents. I use the word "community" to mean the town we lived in as well as the bond formed in the connection between people working and sharing together. Ben's dad was a part of the first Job Corps camp in 1964, a program designed to lift up young people in poverty with training for gainful employment. Sergeant Shriver was his boss. His mother, after moving to Pensacola in the 1970s, became involved in beta Sigma Phi, a women's service sorority. My mom, of course, had her hand in a number of church and civic groups. It was natural that Ben and I would follow in their footsteps.

An opportunity came in the form of marriage preparation for engaged couples in both of our churches. With Benito away at school, we took up leadership in the Catholic Engaged Encounter. This meant Ben and I were responsible for the direction of at least four weekend retreats each year. This included registration, obtaining a site, recruiting, and training married speakers in Tallahassee and Pensacola. We traveled to Mobile AL and Lafayette LA for training and other gatherings. We enjoyed meeting with couples to plan and present weekends which were tailored to meet the needs of engaged couples who wanted to be married in the Catholic Church. The weekend was also a prayerful activity, sprinkled with scheduled quiet time for us to talk to each other about any difficulties we may be having at home, in our marriage, and in our spiritual life.

The work deepened our commitment to each other. I liked being away from the house on retreat and relished the time with Ben away from household distractions. Ben takes up leadership roles easily. He showed me how organized he is with flexibility for unexpected events. While keeping an eye on me and my comfort, we received much love from the couples we served. They laughed at our stories and quirks. Also, they gained a better understanding of each other and their upcoming partnership by attending the weekend retreats.

Likewise in the Methodist Church, we stepped up to develop a program of marriage preparation in Pensacola. We modified the Catholic Engaged Encounter and invited more couples to join us, forming a community. We felt an important connection with our team members. The flow of married love extended to their children and families too. People came to us to be a sounding board for family struggles. Eventually, we expanded to include a parenting class. Ben and I were enjoying stable careers and, at that stage, we found joy in sharing what we knew with these Christian compatriots.

Meanwhile, Ben's mom, Robbie, invited us to her beta Sigma Phi yearly dance. These were big events held in a fancy hotel in downtown Pensacola which included dinner and dancing. Robbie's sorority sisters planned and chose themes for each year's dance. One year the theme was Disney princesses. Robbie chose to dress as Snow White. She dyed her red hair deep brown to match the outfit she had made exactly like the Disney Snow White. I found a bright pink formal to wear at a second-hand store. The night was a blast with a live band and ballroom dancing. Ben and I were taking lessons, so we got to show off a little. The food was excellent, and we had a professional photo taken as a keepsake.

But poor Snow White when the dance was over, tried to wash out the deep brown hair dye. No luck. It was there for good. She was stuck with dark hair with reddish roots for two months.

Robbie oversaw the whole dance in 1998. She chose the theme of Native American women. Ben's dad, Gilbert, was a quarter Native American of the Apache tribe from New Mexico. She researched little known native American women including Sacajawea and Wilma mankiller. Susan La Fleshe Picotte was an early native physician. Maria Tallchief was a prima ballerina. Each sorority sister dressed as a famous Native American woman. To top it off, Robbie invited the local Poarch Creek Indian dancers to entertain at the gala. The room became silent as the two dozen snake dancers processed into the hall in a single line. Every other one held a live snake. Their performance was awe-inspiring as they drummed out a beat and solemnly honored their tradition. Robbie and Gilbert were in their glory.

Whether telling our stories or demonstrating our heritage to a roomful of unsuspecting partygoers, our lives were never dull. Benito traveled with the FSU swim team all over the southeast as their manager. None of us are likely to be the people quietly sitting on the sidelines. We have tried to make our mark to enjoy the life we have received. Maybe some of God's greatest gifts come to us in good times so that we have the grace to draw from when trouble comes.

Our cups overflowing the next year would test our tenacity and resilience. We planned a special party for Gilbert and Robbie's 50th wedding anniversary in June. Then Ben was notified that he was to be in the first class of deacons to be ordained in the United Methodist Church. He had been a diaconal minister for a few years before we met. This meant he served the church in some pastoral duties like reading the scripture or prayers at services. However, his ministry was outside the church as a school counselor. He worked in the world and then brought the world to the church community. He was part of a small group of others with the same designation in the church. But change was coming, and he was part of the wave. He was to be ordained the weekend before the big anniversary party for his parents.

I love parties. I helped send the invitations and discreetly invited out-of-town relatives to surprise Gil and Robbie. But I have these bones that can really spoil plans for a perfect event. On the last day of school, while visiting a student's home in Pensacola, I fell and broke both legs. The ambulance took me to Sacred Heart hospital where Ben met me. They immediately made me comfortable and took X-rays. My orthopedic doctor gazed at the X-rays, shaking his head. I could see with my drugged hazy eyes that this was not going to be an easy operation. Ben had just had a terrible, no-good day, and to make it worse, it was his birthday!

35

Two Legs at a Time

*The real miracle is not to walk either on water
or in thin air, but to walk on earth.*
— Thich nhat Hanh

Ben did not get a cake that year but instead had to spring into action. It was Memorial Day weekend, so while others were purchasing food for cookouts, Ben got on the phone to make arrangements. My mom was to fly in the next morning for a ten-day visit. He needed to contact the Methodist Bishop's office to see if his ordination could be rescheduled and to find someone to build a ramp at our house in Gulf Breeze. One phone call to our friend Karen Evans, another diaconal minister, did the trick. Karen arranged to pick up my mom at the Pensacola airport and bring her to the hospital in the morning. She also knew someone who could build a ramp. Karen was to be ordained with Ben, and it was decided that he could probably make it to Montgomery on Monday if we found another friend to stay with me at the hospital for the day.

After a harrowing night of little sleep, soon after I woke up, I was on my way to the surgical suite. The nurse greeted me with "So do you know what you're here for?"

"If you don't know then I'm not going! How can you ask me that?" I snarked.

Ben was there to urge me to calm down saying, "Mary, she's just making sure you know." But my ire was triggered due to the severe pain and lack of sleep." Then my mother appeared wearing her red blazer with a big smile on her face. Our Methodist minister showed up too. They joined in a quick prayer for my healing, and my bed was rolled into surgery. A pin and screws were placed to hold my left femur in place by Doctor Dennie. I woke up with both legs in splints and a strange pumping device squeezing my feet every few seconds back in my hospital room. My left femur was broken, and my right knee had a break as well. It was hard to believe I'd be able to walk again.

I kept calling my boss so I could tell her what happened. When I reached her, I learned that since the injury occurred while I was making a home visit to a client, Workers' Compensation would pay the costs. I was supposed to go to Baptist Hospital which was affiliated with our agency. Oops! Eventually, we worked out that Doctor Dennie could continue to follow my treatment.

Ben was ordained as planned. My mom, Benito, and his family got to enjoy the celebration in Montgomery. My healing was lifted in prayer by all those in attendance.

The following weekend, we hosted the surprise 50th wedding anniversary party for Ben's parents as we had planned. We rented the Methodist Church Hall and arranged for them to be transported to the hall in a limousine. Upon arrival, they were greeted by a mariachi band. Robbie's sister and her children came in from Maryland. It made my heart leap for joy to see how much they enjoyed these surprises. I sat in my wheelchair and forgot all my pain. Ben's brothers and sister helped make the party a huge success. The band played, and people danced. All her sorority sisters shared in the celebration. After the church reception, family and sorority sisters came to our backyard for a fish fry. We had a local favorite fried mullet and all the fixings catered by Chet"s seafood, one of their favorite restaurants. Chet brought their food truck and cooked it all in our driveway. Perhaps this was the first food truck anniversary party ever in Gulf Breeze! Ben's sister, Teresa, and my mom and I had made the pinatas by hand the day before.

What a night! The party lasted until the moon rose over the Live Oak trees in our yard. I retired to the bedroom while Gil and Robbie opened presents. We had done it! Somehow the party was a success despite my two broken legs. Ben showed his ability to take the lead in a big project. He was unflappable. A man of few words, he agreed everything went well and all was "Okay."

"Now let's focus on getting you well," Ben insisted.

Ben was off work for the summer so he could take care of me. I was not able to bend either leg as both were in splints. I had to get around in a wheelchair with both legs stuck out in front. As you can imagine, this made riding in the car quite difficult. We worked out a system to use a board to slide into the back seat, sitting sideways. It was a long, hot summer. Benito got a summer job in Tallahassee, so I slept in his room for a while. We had just purchased a futon, and when folded out, it was low enough for me to scoot myself into the bed from the wheelchair.

Ben was on duty 24 hours a day! We spent the time playing games and watching movies. I read and received visitors. On good days, Ben wheeled my chair out into the driveway. Our dog, Susie, kept me company. It would be a long time before I could perform any chores in the house, which I didn't mind. Some days Ben took me to the swimming pool at the university of West Florida where there was a lift to get me into the pool. I was able to swim before I could walk. In the water I was free. I made a little booklet about the gripping discomfort of broken bones, drawing them and illustrating the colors of pain. Art therapy again.

By August, school was about to begin. I returned to Belleview Middle School in a wheelchair with transportation paid for by Workers' Comp. It wasn't so bad because the hallways were smooth, and they gave me room in the guidance office to see students. I could wheel myself, but it was always fun to let the middle school boys push me down the hall fast and furiously. I realized being in a wheelchair was good for rapport to be at eye level with the kids; they talked to me more easily. At the same time, I was getting physical therapy. By Christmas, I was able to walk again.

What did I learn from all this? That I am loved. Ben demonstrated this to me every day by dressing me, feeding me, listening to me, and loving me. Friends were dear; Sherrye bathed my feet; Catherine brought me impatiens flowers planted in a bedpan. Ironic. Neighbors brought food. Greeting cards brought daily joy. I was determined to walk more carefully and take better care of myself. As soon as I could, I restarted my gentle yoga practice.

Recovery is not easy, but it does come.

36

Mind, Body, Spirit

*Mystics look out from different eyes
what they see is the grace in all things,
the deep connection between things.*
— R. Rohr

Once I picked up a table from a coworker to donate to one of my clients. Upon loading it onto Ben's truck, he said "What makes you have such a glowing spirit?"

I said, "Maybe it's because I practice yoga."

Ben and I have always thought fitness was important. Ben joined Chip's Gym in Gulf Breeze, and I accompanied him as a guest. He lifted weights, and I rode a stationary bike. It helped me to strengthen my legs after the fractures. Eventually, we noticed there was a yoga class in the evenings, so we started to attend. We had to squeeze ourselves in between the workout machines in the women's section. About a dozen people of all sizes and strengths showed up for yoga every Tuesday and Thursday. This met our need for a good stretch and helped me to strengthen other parts of my body. With my crooked arm and stiff joints, I can't say I was the poster child for yoga, but I kept at it and found it was a great stress reliever. My mind was so taken up with getting into the poses (asanas) that I didn't have time to worry about things that bothered me. Ben really liked it too.

At the same time, we became interested in the study of theology at Spring Hill College in Mobile AL, just an hour from our home. Spring Hill College is referred to as the Fordham of the South, a Jesuit college with summer and graduate programs in spirituality. Ben and I both attended their summer classes and our spiritual life improved because of it. The Jesuits are known for their educational standards. I took a class on the Desert Fathers taught by William Harmless, S.J. who had studied original documents from the 3rd century. Ben found enrichment in a class on the Holy Spirit by another visiting Jesuit professor. Eventually, Ben decided to enroll in a two-year program of Jesuit spirituality to become a spiritual director in that tradition. Ben loves to study and works hard in an educational setting. This program really met his need for serious study and growth in spirituality. He made several silent retreats during the two years. The class included many readings and seminars, and he had clients in Mobile to practice his new skill.

We knew God was drawing us closer in both practices, yoga and spiritual direction. We had completed our work with marriage preparation, so these were new ways to work and grow together. We met new friends. We read books on Saint Ignatius, founder of the Jesuits in the 16th century.

If that was not enough when he completed that course, Ben decided to become a yoga instructor himself. He traveled to Fort Walton Beach FL, an hour east, one weekend a month for a year. Ben is a lifelong learner and as long as I was healthy, he could be away from home for short times. I learned many things along with Ben and read some of the same books he was learning from.

After Benito graduated from FSU, he moved to Orlando FL to take a job with the YMCA. He was enjoying his single life, along with driving his own new Chevy truck. He worked hard, even transferring to the Tampa YMCA for a year. Then he fell in love. He met Julie who was working at the YMCA in the summers while attending the University of Florida. This was no light romance. They broke up for a while, but shortly after Ben's mother Robbie died, Julie made her way back to Benito, and they moved in together, setting a wedding date for 2004.

Their wedding was one for the ages. Julie is Jewish, one of three children born and raised in Orlando. Her father is in real estate, and her mother was a guidance counselor in the Orange County schools. Considering this, they had both a Jewish rabbi and a Methodist minister officiated at the ceremony. Ben's dad and my mom were part of the procession. This was a big wedding with dinner and dancing. It was at the Isleworth Country Club where Tiger Woods lived at the time. Both Julie and Benito liked nice things and dressing up. Some of my sisters and my brother came to Florida for the event as well as Ben's brothers and sister. My dress cost more than I'd like to admit, but I looked fabulous. After the wedding, Julie and Benito settled into their lives in Orlando.

Things were status quo back in Gulf Breeze. I took a different job at Lakeview Center, one that didn't involve driving and carrying my stuff from school to school. Ben changed schools as well. We continued our yoga practice and Ben started to teach at the studio occasionally. We had many happy times.

After Robbie's death, Ben's dad was alone. He became more involved in the Lions Club and traveled to various conventions. When his health started to fail, we moved him out of his house in Pensacola and rented a house for him across the street from ours. We had a great relationship. He loved me and told me his stories about World War II and his life growing up in New Mexico. Ben said he never talked so much to anyone but me. He loved women! He had wanted six children, all girls, but instead, he got five sons and one daughter. He loved to kid me about my poor cooking ability as he and Robbie were both good cooks.

I wrote about my yoga practice that was published in a book of alternative psalms put together by people from First United Methodist Church in Pensacola, *A Living Psalter*. My yoga practice began to feel like prayer. Yoga in a group begins to feel like group prayer. The actions in this poem fit the sun salutation a set of yoga moves.

My body praises you!
I stretch my hands up-reaching.
Pull me up to you, oh God.
I place my arms together,
Pointed up to the heavens.
I stretch high my fingers
To show my longing and desire
To reach you - to offer you myself
I lift myself to your sky
I lift my head out of my chest
And into your light.
And then I bow
I bend deep to honor you
And to humble myself
like a warrior before a king
A knight ready for service
I bend my knee
and lower my head to you
And standing again, chest open
Heart forward
Be within me
My heart's quickened beat
Sound for you my Lord
and behold all that has
already been given me us
To us, Ben and me, each other
Thank you for my family of birth
And families of faith
For our new heartbeat in Julie's womb
for the gift of life
we glorify your name.
We lift our hearts to you
As it is only fitting and wise
you are within each breath.
we bring our bodies to prayer
Our minds to you we bend
for our cares our many
before us all the day
Conflicts, secrets, plans, futures
Before us they stride.
We carry our hands and feet

but no they are yours.
We ask for a contrite and humble heart
to do your will.
We ask to be makers of the Kingdom
workers in the vineyard
planters in the garden
merciful lenders
and forgive us our transgressions.
We bring our bodies to prayer
We bring our burdens and place them before you
As in the days of old.
we know we are not alone.
we sense that you have a mission
we hope that you will live in us.
With a contrite heart and humble spirit
let this prayer be received!

<h1 style="text-align:center">37</h1>

Bubble Wrap is Holding

We tried to sleep but outside the wind and rain howled. Our cat, Dusty was all over the bed as we feigned sleep. We had no electricity that night nor water the next morning. In the morning we looked outside to see the destruction of trees and parts of houses strewn up and down the street. Only the battery-operated radio alerted us to the dangerous travel conditions and devastation. Cell towers were down, and we had no way to power the phone. And since it was September, the temperature in Florida was in the 80s and 90s. Some people in the neighborhood set up generators for power but we didn't have one. This was Hurricane Ivan, in 2004. That year Florida had four hurricanes hit our state. Hurricane Ivan hit the Pensacola area leaving 14 dead. This storm was so large at Category 3 or 5 depending on where it struck. Deaths occurred in North Carolina and Georgia, too.

Thank goodness we were safe. This time, we had left Gulf Breeze situated on a thin peninsula South of Pensacola, and evacuated to Ben's dad's house in Pensacola. Gilbert was in New Mexico, so he missed all the fun. It was fortunate we got over the three-mile bridge before it closed.

We purchased a vacation cabin in the north Georgia mountains in 2002. So, after two nights without water or electricity, we decided to leave town and drove to our cabin in Georgia. All along the way, we could follow the path of the storm. There were trees down in Alabama and Georgia. When we arrived at our cabin, there was no electricity, but the temperature was much more comfortable. We were so tired we fell into bed. The next day we got power again. We stayed a week and were able to reach our bosses and family members by phone. Schools were closed. My agency was closed. Our families were quite worried, however. Ben's brother, Jeff, in Virginia, told us he watched the

TV coverage of the storm all night. He said at one point there were no transmissions going in or out of Pensacola. He was quite worried. We were able to assure them all we were fine.

Returning to work, I had two grieving employees who lost their homes completely. School was closed for three weeks. We spent time checking on clients to make sure they had food even if they didn't have electricity. It was a sad time. I would meet people at the store or on the street and hear their stories of fear and loss. Many were surviving on government meals called MREs or meals-ready-to-eat. And many were displaced, living with friends or in FEMA trailers set up in parking lots. Debris of tree limbs, roofs, appliances, clothing, and more piled up on every street. There was the stench of rotting life everywhere. In October, I flew to Ohio for my nephew's wedding. As the plane took off from the Pensacola airport, I was shocked to see how many roofs were still covered with blue FEMA blue tarps.

As time went on, our cabin life in Ellijay GA was looking better and better. When we sat on the porch or set a fire in the fireplace, we felt real peace. We met our neighbors. We discovered hiking trails. And when it was time to go back to Florida, I felt the old familiar pit in my stomach of not wanting to leave. It wasn't our time to slow down. Not yet. I changed positions again at Lakeview Center, out of the school for difficult students and into an administrative job still helping children. And the best news of all in those years was that Julie and Benito were having their first child.

Embe was born on May 13th, 2007, Mother's Day. I felt I had finally joined the human race because of that child. I was a grandmother! My new title became Mimi. My heart bounced with somersaults. We let the new parents be and finally met Embe in June when school was out. Pictures galore filled our home, and some became dog-eared in my purse. We thanked God for a healthy child.

Esther dragged her oxygen chord all over the house. At 87, she wasn't done yet. Esther was one of Gilberts' three surviving siblings. Ben's dad was one of sixteen children. Gilbert's sisters, Esther and Aurelia, were still alive. We met them both on an extended vacation to New Mexico in 2008. I noticed that at each Encinias home, there was a bullfighter of some sort on their walls or in sculpture form, depicting their Spanish heritage.

Gilbert's brother, Miguel Encinias, was also living in Albuquerque. He had become a professor of history and French at the University of New Mexico. This was after an extensive career in the Air Force as a pilot. He was in WWII, the Korean War, and in Vietnam as an advisor. We knew him from his visits to Pensacola. Miguel knew New Mexico like a woodworker knows wood. He guided us to many historic places including their childhood home in Las Vegas NM. Miquel and Gilbert were just two of the youngest boys of the sixteen children. We soaked up the history of this remarkable family in our visit.

Taking in the beauty of Santa Fe and Taos was astonishing. We were stunned by the natural beauty and the art of Georgia O'Keefe. I was inspired to paint and to write again. In Taos, we were able to practice yoga, and I found a Recreation Center with a pool in which to swim. I was in my glory. In addition, I noticed that everyone in Albuquerque looked or walked like Ben. He was in his native land feeling quite comfortable.

We returned to Florida to take up our careers and started making plans to retire when Ben turned 64.

38

Tripple Whammy

In August 2008, I met the most handsome surgeon ever made. This was after an ambulance ride in which I was cared for by two young EMTs. Doctor Handsome looked at me with kind brown eyes. I was lying on a bed in the ER of a Baptist hospital. Although I was in extreme pain, I was willing to talk to this doctor and explain what got me there. I had a bad fall. It happened at a funeral for my friend, Peggy's husband. Peggy and I had worked together in adoptions, and there were families in the church we knew from our work. The church was crowded. So naturally after the service, I wanted to join the reception in the church hall. While talking with one of the families, I missed a step and fell with arms facing forward. One leg was twisted under my body, so I knew right away I had broken both arms and one leg.

The handsome doctor was on loan from the military doing a rotation on trauma surgery. We found out later, he was one of the ten most eligible men in America in Ebony magazine in 2008. That evening, once he found his favorite shoes for doing surgery, he put a pin inside my right femur and set both arms in casts. Ben waited with me for him to be ready in the surgical suite, which seemed like an eternity. And then I woke up. I endured horrible pain throughout the night, but the sun came up in the morning. Ben gently gave me a sponge bath, and my sister, Maggie, and her husband arrived from Maryland to cheer me into my recovery.

We were told I was in a very special room. If I looked out the window, I could see a wooden door stuck up in an old oak tree from Hurricane Ivan five years ago. Everyone in Pensacola remembered Ivan so this was a bittersweet token of that terrible storm. It gave me something to share with my many visitors. I had lots of visitors including the minister who delivered the eulogy at the fated funeral. After three days in the hospital, I was sent to a rehab facility.

Life at the rehab facility was rough for three months from August to November. Ben never could have taken care of me at home with both arms broken; I couldn't feed myself nor walk. The physical therapists fabricated a special walker for me with shoulder-level rests for my arms. Within a few days, I was able to walk on my own with this contraption throughout the halls of the facility. I need it so much! My best friend, Sherrye, made me muumuus that were easy to take off and on with Velcro strips up the side. Friends and sometimes staff members had to feed me three times a day. I laid there with my two arms useless. It was hard to blow my nose and put on my glasses. The pain was relentless. The titanium pin in my leg was wreaking havoc on my nerve cells. The head nurse had to closely monitor my pain medication which was a highly controlled drug. The care was moderately good, but every facility like this is understaffed. There were times when my assigned nurse was busy with another patient in another room, and I couldn't get help.

The emotions I felt were intense. I woke up every day depressed that I was still in the facility. I got a shower only every three days. It was unnerving to let someone else wash my face and bottom. One nurse's aide introduced herself, "I'm Katrina, Category Five!" A tribute to the devastating hurricane that hit New Orleans. She came into my room once and announced that she didn't have time to give me a full bath, but she would just wash my face and my "pocketbook." You can figure out what she meant.

I slept well until I was awakened in the middle of the night by the nurse on duty to check for bed sores. I know now that the bed check was mandatory. But I was up and out of bed every day for physical therapy; there was no chance I would get a bed sore. This experience was the worst to date of all my fractures and recovery.

On the positive side, everything was covered by insurance, and I had plenty of sick leave to keep my paycheck coming. I had visitors every day. Ben cut back his work schedule to three days a week because if I had a doctor's appointment, he had to get me there. Rehab centers don't have doctors. Let that sink in. Ben came every day during those long weeks. I went through seven roommates. I think I'm easy to get along with, but one roommate wanted me out. She was a long-term resident with mental limitations and a crush on one of the male nurses. She watched true crime stories all day long on the television. I felt schooled in murder by the time she moved out. If I could have used my arms, I might have considered killing a few people myself. Some days, I had no roommates which was great. I felt free to listen to music and talk on the phone without someone hearing me. Several of the residents were there for therapy following knee replacements. We laughed and sang together in the therapy room just to help the time go by. I love my show tunes.

In October the casts came off my arms, but my arms were so weak I couldn't even peel a banana. It was a time of extreme disappointment and fear. My hands and fingers were OK, but I had no strength in my arms at all. Neither elbow would bend so they provided long rubber-coated silverware to feed myself. It was a sight!

Ben and others brought me treats all the time. For my birthday, we had a steak dinner on the patio. I lived from pill to pill and visit to visit. Each one of my sisters came from out of town for a week. They stayed with Ben at our house; then using my car, they visited me in rehab all day long. What a gift! Anne came from Pittsburgh; Rita and her husband Tom came from Cleveland around Halloween. They brought a Halloween cake and a light-up pumpkin which cheered me immensely. During their visit, they agreed to take me to my dental appointment. It was great to get out of the rehab center and by that time, I could sit in a car. That was weird being rolled up a ramp rarely used at the small dentist's office. As far as brushing my teeth, I couldn't do it myself. This was a dental cleaning for the best hygienist.

I felt embarrassed at the condition of my teeth, but she did not seem to mind and prattled on about her latest dates. I was relieved when it was over. Then we went out for dinner at our favorite Cajun place. It was going to be a long recovery.

As with other fractures, I was surrounded by people who cared. Every week a woman from a local church brought me holy communion. I had visits from priests and pastoral care people from the Methodist Church. I tried to keep my spirits up, but I needed this attention from others to get through those long days.

Do you know who Troy Aikman is? He's a former NFL star quarterback for the Dallas Cowboys. We have a connection. By January 2009, my left arm was still weak and painful. I was referred to an orthopedic surgeon who was an arm and hand specialist. He diagnosed a non-union fracture; one in which the bones are not growing back together. This was my left arm! I use it for everything! Doctor Coleman decided to do outpatient surgery to repair the bone. I was ready to get it done. He had previously worked in sports medicine operating on Troy Aikman. Maybe someday I'll be able to throw a football, too.

Also, in January, I was permitted to work from home and to hire another counselor to assist with the work. The program I administered had been on hold while I was in rehab. I was responsible for thirty children's mental health care under a special state program. It was hard to see 1000 unopened emails in my inbox, but little by little, I went through them. Ben set up a pile of soft foam which cradled my arms as I typed. I could make phone calls with a speaker phone. Little by little I got back into the work. My new colleague, Pat, was able to do the driving. We had to interview new clients which took us to Fort Walton Beach and DeFuniak Springs, Florida in the Panhandle. It wasn't until April that I felt comfortable driving again.

One of my go-to coping skills is humor. My brain works overtime making connections and word play, even during staff meetings. Sometimes I need to tone it down because I have learned that one must never be funnier than the boss. I'm a jokester. I can't deny it. Humor has helped me put people at ease my whole life. I can sense when people are uncomfortable around me. Most of the time, a little light humor is welcomed in mental health work. We had needy clients and became drained ourselves if we took things too seriously. And in addition to healing, we had something else to celebrate. Benito and Julie had their second child on the last day of December; a healthy boy, Tollan, who will always have a big party on his birthday, New Year's Eve.

39

Goodbyes

It was the last straw. My mom had continued to share her home in Ohio with those who were down and out. But in the last few years she had some hangers-on who had more problems than mom could handle. One fellow was a petty thief with a criminal record. He brought Mom trinkets from his wandering around town; small statues, artificial flowers, whatever he found. Mom enjoyed his lively personality. Another young man helped every week to serve the hot meal at Saint Mary's. He had always kept his bedroom door closed, and Mom respected his privacy. The third man, Louie, was autistic. He assembled computer parts as a hobby. He put a camera in the upstairs hallway and kept a lock on the door. Each of these characters brought some joy and their own heartache to the house. Louie discovered that the hot meal guy was drinking and smoking in his room. Once the door was opened, whiskey bottles and ashtrays were found. Our childhood home was becoming a flophouse.

Marg, Rita, Anne and I enlisted the help of our big brother, Jim. He met with the men to ask them to clear out. They had brought lice and bedbugs to the house. Mom was now in her 90s. She was naive and too forgiving. We siblings started to talk to her about assisted living or nursing home care.

Jim gave them a week to get other accommodations. Louis stuck around but set up a tent in the backyard where he slept. He couldn't take the bedbugs. Mom never complained. My sister Rita and her husband Tom did what they could to monitor what was going on, but they lived twenty minutes away and visited at least once a week to steam her mattress, couch, and chair to keep down the bedbugs. We burned up the telephone lines trying to fix a problem that had gotten out of hand. At 93, she was still driving to church for Mass each morning. She lost her purse, including her license and bank card, several times. When her car broke down, we didn't get it fixed. She started to call friends for a ride to church or walk there herself, eight blocks. The last Christmas that I visited her in her home, Louie was still around. But I could see her decline. Finally, with the efforts of Rita and Tom. myself and her doctor, we got her a room in Wesleyan Manor, a nursing home on West Avenue in Elyria.

Wesleyan Manor is only about six blocks from her home, and she had visited there many times, helping the old people attend the monthly mass in the auditorium. In her new room, she could see the steeple of Saint Mary's. She yearned to go there for services. But the one time Rita took her to church, Mom was unable to understand or keep up with the mass. Her mind couldn't focus. Over the next three years, she looked after her roommates at the home. She answered their phones, blessed them with holy water while they slept, and made sure each one had napkins and silverware at their place setting in the dining room. Mom was a giver until her death in 2015. She kept a list and a photo album of all the people who lived with her in our house on 12th St. We found there were over 100 names on that list!

She was a great woman, inspired by Dorothy Day as I had been so many years ago. Her funeral was in the dead of winter; Elyria was covered in snow. Our family mourned and celebrated her life. The local newspaper printed an article about her on the front page. We showed off all the awards she received over the years from volunteer organizations and the Diocese of Cleveland. There would never be another person like her.

At the same time, Ben was nearing retirement. Our little cabin in North Georgia was our place of refuge and rest. We traveled there about seven hours from home. At least twice a year. It was getting harder and harder to come back to our busy Pensacola life. Ben had been planning for his retirement for many years. He had projects in mind: woodworking, art pieces, and crafting ideas. As most teachers do, he kept everything and gleaned office supplies from school which were to be discarded. He was ready to let go of responsibilities and live in the mountains full-time.

By 2011, he could leave the school system with a fair retirement income. We liked the small-town atmosphere of Ellijay and Blue Ridge, GA. We liked hiking. In the foothills of the Appalachian Mountains. So, we retired to the mountains.

Ben's last day of work was May 23, 2011. The elementary school in which he served planned a nice retirement luncheon for him at the school cafeteria. They all knew his plan was to live in the mountains and teach yoga. It was a fitting sendoff for this simple quiet man who had worked since his teens. He needed no fanfare.

We were just ready to turn the page.

40

Cabin in the Woods

*The moment one definitely commits
oneself, then Providence moves, too.
All sorts of things occur to help one that would never
otherwise have occurred. A whole stream of events
issues from the decision which no one would have
dreamed would have come their way.*
W.H. Murray

A surprise hoedown party was held for me as I left Lakeview. All my colleagues dressed as hillbillies to prepare me for living in rural Georgia. They had bluegrass music playing. Some wore overalls and blacked out their teeth. It was a hoot. I sat in a rocking chair and opened presents such as mouse traps, country music CDs, and a straw hat. Overhead was a video showing photos of our many good times together. Because of HIPPA, the privacy law, it wasn't allowed to invite or say goodbye to clients in this way. I had my individual farewells with them. So many come to mind. I loved many of them. We shared tough times together.

I was ready to say goodbye to Pensacola. Goodbye to the life of work and paychecks. Goodbye to garbage collection and groceries just five minutes away. Goodbye to walks in the neighborhood with live oaks and Spanish moss. Goodbye to Driftwood Lane, our Gulf Breeze address. Goodbye to dyed-blonde retirees. Goodbye to the Three Mile Bridge, the delays and the trucks after Hurricane Ivan. Goodbye to Pensacola Beach, the restaurants, the parades, the bars, the hotels. Goodbye to the gulf, those warm, salty waters that toss me like a washing machine. Goodbye to long afternoons in the sun covered with sticky sand. Goodbye to noisy lawnmowers and A/C units. Goodbye to the unrelenting heat of August and September to the steering wheels you could not touch, closed windows, and prickly pear. Goodbye to elephant ears, holly, crepe myrtle, and Jerusalem cherry. Goodbye to Lakeview where I worked for 15 years. Goodbye to treatment plans and performance reviews. Goodbye to dressing up. Picking out an outfit, smiling at grumpy receptionists. Goodbye to traffic lights, sirens, smooth roads, hurricanes. Goodbye to elevators and parking lots full of hot cars. Goodbye to clients who were just people before I met them. Goodbye to diagnosis and global assessments of functioning. Goodbye to family histories, Social Security numbers, shot records, soccer dues, excel worksheets, eligibility requirements, arrest records, medical needs, shredding the records so painstakingly gathered. Goodbye to meetings, agendas, calendars, and Venn diagrams.

Parting with dear friends was difficult. I had lived in Pensacola for nearly 25 years. We had been present for the deaths of both of Ben's parents whose ashes remain at the National graveyard at Naval Air Station in Pensacola. We met and married here. This was Benito's hometown. Considering this, it was an emotional move, but also one with hope for an exciting new chapter.

We were eager to settle in Blue Ridge. We did all the necessary things such as getting new driver's licenses and fitting all our stuff into the small cabin. This took time. My leg pain was quite bad, probably a hairline fracture. But I didn't get an X-ray. We found a family Doctor who had a patient previously with OI, so that made me feel better. I had hoped to seek out work in the area but was unable to walk much because of the pain. So instead, I applied for Social Security Disability. I was only 59 years old. I had to go to various doctors for evaluation. One day while Ben was out, I struggled out of bed to answer the phone. It was Social Security asking for a former doctor's phone number. They could hear the level of pain in my voice as I looked for the information they sought. After X-rays of my arms and legs and a review of all my past medical records, I was approved for disability in May 2012. I was now free to just take care of myself and live the life I wanted. It was a good feeling. After all. I had worked for thirty years. Like Ben, I had things I wanted to do.

We now live on a forested hill twenty miles from town in northern Georgia. Wildlife surrounds us every day. We see bunnies, deer, squirrels, and birds. And once a young bear. Driving in our area around curves up and down hills, we see cattle and large chicken farms. In the summer, butterflies, moths, and lightning bugs join us. We smell wood burning on some days. The gunshots of hunters and those who do target practice unnerve us, but it is rare. We have entered the quiet silence of a simpler life. We are happy.

A pie in the face. A hunk of straw on my shoulder. A leopard print dress with bangles. A nosy neighbor. What do these things have in common? It's community theater. Who knew I could start an acting career in my 60s? The first audition netted a part. I was thrilled. I was terrified. Will the audience notice my crooked arm? Will I remember my lines? Will I trip during the chase scene?

I didn't. I excelled and loved the attention. Never nervous. I put on my costume and played a church lady more than once. One loved, one hated. Hence the pie scene was carefully choreographed to surprise the audience. Twelve times. Twelve performances. Thus, my life in the mountains was no quiet life. Instead, it became a riot of new friends, new faces, and new experiences.

Ben became interested in crafting props. He worked determinedly to make a Falcon with a radio antenna. He made tombstones, bones, and three-foot rocks out of paper mache'. We began to appreciate opening nights and final bows. I slept like a rock. I somehow endured eight different roles in six years. It was thrilling and exhausting.

Meanwhile, our third grandchild was born. Benito and his family visited us up in the mountains at least once a year. Hiking, dunking each other in the hot tub, and tracking snails in the woods are some of our activities. We couldn't be happier.

Yes, the bones still break. Ben taught yoga for three years here in North Georgia. I'm sure my yoga practice kept me limber for a while. But I'm finally slowing down. I have arthritis in my shoulder and bursitis in my hip, but I am able to walk. The Blue Ridge Poets and Writers Group have inspired and challenged me to complete this book. I saw a bumper sticker yesterday that said "Courage to get started, strength to finish." I have learned so much through these years. I'm thankful for my family, for Ben and for the urge to tell my story. All is well.

Happiness is a choice.

What is Osteogenesis Imperfecta?

Breaking Down Brittle Bones

Let me explain this in simple terms, give you a quick history of the disorder, what's going on biologically in the body and some treatment options.

What is Osteogenesis Imperfecta? The actual words, 'osteogenesis imperfecta', just as many other medical terms, have their roots in the Latin language. Osteogenesis imperfecta literally means IMPERFECT BONE FORMATION. Pretty simple, right? This is a hereditary disorder, caused by collagen abnormality that ultimately causes fragility of the skeleton and deformity of the bones. Since it is a collagen disorder, and the entire body is made up of collagen, many other organs of the body can be affected: the heart, lungs, and other organs. Even though O.I. is a hereditary disorder, there have been cases of spontaneous mutations occurring for people with O.I.

With that said, O.I. is classified as a rare disease. In the United States, in order for a disease to be classified as rare, the number of affected people needs to be under 200,000. O.I. affects between 25,000 and 40,000 persons in the United States (1 in every 10,000 people). There is such a wide gap in these statistics due to the fact that some of the less severe cases of O.I. go undetected and are not recorded.

The basic characteristics of O.I. include but are not limited to;

- Multiple broken bones from non-traumatic events – This means breaking bones from doing simple, everyday tasks or movements. Everything from lifting something to stepping and landing your foot in a weird way.

- Blue sclera – the white around our eye is called the

sclera. When someone has O.I. the white can have a blue tint to it. This doesn't occur in everyone with O.I. and can depend on the severity.

- Short stature. Some types of O.I. are dwarf, but the majority of O.I.ers are shorter than average.

- Deformities – the majority of persons with O.I., even in the mildest cases, will have some sort of deformity. It may not always be visible or noticeable, but for the most part this does occur. With more severe cases, the deformities can be very extreme and cause or create issues with mobility and other bodily functions.

According to Dr. Eric T. Rush, Assistant Professor of Pediatrics, Internal Medicine and Orthopedic Surgery at the University of Nebraska Medical Center, there are 18 types of O.I. based on the combination of molecular and/or phenotypic distinctions. The Types are not classified by severity, but by this mutation type. What this means is that the classifications are not in sequential order based on severity. Type I is mild, while Type II is the most severe and deadliest form. Type III is severe, and Type IV is closer to Type I, and so on. I had genetic testing, and it was reported that I am Type V.

There is evidence in medical literature of a fragile bones disorder dating back to ancient Egyptian times. There are bones of an Egyptian child dated somewhere around 1,000 B.C. that have signs that the child may have had fragile bones due to the stature and deformities in the bones. Also, there was a man called Ivar the Boneless who was a great warrior and army leader in 850 A.D. He was said to be very short in stature and to break his bones easily.

The term "Osteogenesis Imperfecta" was first used in the Handbook of Pathological Anatomy, written in 1849, by Willem Vrolik, Professor of Anatomy at the University of Amsterdam.

So what does O.I. do in the body – how does it work biologically? In normal bone formation, collagen, which is a protein, is produced by the body and begins to braid together. Thee braids then stack together to form the bone matrix. We can think of the bone matrix as the framework. Once the bone matrix is complete, two other cells come in to play: osteoblasts and osteoclasts. Osteoblasts are the cells that make more bone within the bone matrix by attaching and filling in the framework. Osteoclasts, on the other hand, take bone away This process of creating bone and taking bone away is known as remodeling. Our bodies are constantly involved in this process.

In someone with O.I., the defect starts at the collagen level. The braid of the collagen is malformed. Because of this, the collagen stacks up, and the framework becomes unstable. With an unstable framework, the osteoblasts don't have a solid place to attach to, so new bone cannot be formed. No matter how many new osteoblasts are introduced, there simply won't be a suitable foundation for them to create the new bone.

That's why people suggest – and thank you for your concern- that someone with O.I. should just "Drink more milk!" or "Take extra calcium supplements!" that's not necessarily going to help us.

At the writing of this book, there is no cure for O.I. The main focus and concern is to reduce fracture rate and increase bone density as much as possible. One treatment has been to introduce Biophosphonates, which assists in decreasing bone loss by taking away or disabling the osteoclasts, the cells that take bone away, to give more room for the osteoblasts to create more bone. This treatment has shown good results in children with O.I., but it's not the end-all and it doesn't work with everyone.

Another treatment is using hardware. Inserting rods, plates, and screws to hold bones together has been very successful for many people with O.I. These help to keep the bone in place when a fracture occurs, which in turn helps to expedite the healing time.

Resources

Organizations:

Osteogenesis Imperfecta Foundation https://oif.org

Dorothy Day: www.dorothydayguild.org

The Catholic Worker 36 E. First St., New York City, N.Y. 10003 (212)254-1640

L'Arche community www.larcheusa.org

Our Lady of the Wayside www.thewayside.org

Jesuit Volunteer Corps, 801 Saint Paul St., Baltimore, MD 21202 (410) 244-1733 https://jesuitvolunteers.org

Books:

Abbot, Jim Imperfection Ballantine Books

Heumann, Judith, Being Heumann An Unrepentant Memoir of a Disability Rights Activist, 2020 Beacon Press

Furlong, Monica, Merton: A Biography, 1980, Harper & Row

Jacobsen, Tony, Disable Your Disability Live the Healthy Life You Deserve

Merton, Thomas, The Seven Story Mountain, 1948, Harcourt Brace

Merton, Thomas, Conjectures of a Guilty Bystander, 1968, Image

Miller, William D. A Harsh and Dreadful Love: Dorothy Day and the Catholic Worker Movement, 1974, Image Books

Loaves and Fishes: The Inspiring Story of the Catholic Worker Movement Orbis Books; 1977

Acknowledgments

A big Thank You to early readers Brent Warberg, Roberta Bondi, Tom and Rita Koberna, Tom Peters, Anne Rascov, Maggie Quinlan, Denise Allocca, David Gauchat, Sukoshi Rice, Sherrye Gilman, Paula Miller, Julia Senette, Katherine Oatis, Martha Day Boesel, Martha Hodge, Sally Pamplin, and Lucy Harris.

Dixieanne Hallaj, Short and Helpful (a writing course) helped me with the first part. Carol Crawford was an early editor. Maggie Bruehl helped me get to the finish line. The members of Blue Ridge Mountain Arts, Poets and Writer's Group kept me going.

Lest I forget my intrepid partner, Ben, who loves me when I'm up and when I'm down. He is the introvert to my extravert, the quiet to my noise and the love of my heart.